Children's literature and computer-based teaching

Children's literature and computer-based teaching

Len Unsworth, Angela Thomas,
Alyson Simpson and Jennifer L. Asha

Open University Press

Open University Press
McGraw-Hill Education
McGraw-Hill House
Shoppenhangers Road
Maidenhead
Berkshire
England
SL6 2QL

email: enquiries@openup.co.uk
world wide web: www.openup.co.uk

and Two Penn Plaza, New York, NY 10121-2289, USA

First published 2005

A catalogue record of this book is available from the British Library

ISBN 0 335 21636 6 (pb)   0 335 21637 4 (hb)

Library of Congress Cataloging-in-Publication Data
CIP data applied for

Typeset by RefineCatch Limited, Bungay, Suffolk
Printed in the UK by Bell and Bain Ltd, Glasgow

Contents

About the authors

Jenny Asha is a primary school teacher experienced in teaching gifted and talented children as well as those with learning difficulties. She holds a Master's degree in English and Literacy Education and shares her passion for conventional and computer-based literacies as a guest lecturer and conference speaker. As president of an Australian Literacy Educators Association local council, she leads a group of teachers and librarians interested in promoting the use of conventional and electronic children's literature in the primary classroom.

Alyson Simpson is a lecturer in Primary English and Literacy Education in the Faculty of Education at the University of Sydney. Alyson is an experienced classroom teacher, teacher librarian and researcher. Her research projects include an investigation of the pedagogy of book raps, an exploration of visual literacy in primary schools and an examination of multimodal learning environments.

Angela Thomas is a lecturer in Primary English and Literacy education in the Faculty of Education at the University of Sydney. Angela is an experienced classroom teacher, educational consultant and research project manager. She is the coordinator of the Electronic Literature and Literacies in International Education (ELLIE) project and website in the Faculty of Education, where she teaches in the Bachelor of Education (Primary) and Master of Education programmes.

Len Unsworth is Professor in English and Literacies Education at the University of New England in Armidale, Australia. Len was a classroom teacher in Queensland before moving into teacher education at the University of Western Sydney, and then the University of Sydney prior to taking up his present position. His publications include *Literacy Learning and Teaching* (Macmillan, 1993), *Researching Language in Schools and Communities* (Continuum, 2000) and *Teaching Multiliteracies across the Curriculum* (Open University Press, 2001).

Acknowledgements

We would very much like to express our deep gratitude and thanks to the on-line palace community of Middle Earth. In particular, the owner of the palace, Laurie Sorenson, has been extremely generous in inviting teachers to bring their classes of children onto the palace, and in preparing a special section of the palace for this purpose. She has spent long hours in consultation with the authors of this book in planning the research project outlined in Chapter 6. We are also deeply indebted to the computer programmer of the palace, Russel Dell, who listened to the creative ideas for the role-playing and then wrote sections of complex programming to turn these ideas into reality. A special thank you is also extended to Lin Ahearn, who has spent time teaching us Elvish and preparing avatars for the research project. These three members of the Middle Earth community were also responsible for preparing custom software for our purpose at no charge (available for free download from the ELLIE website (http://sirius.linknet.com.au/ellie/) or from the accompanying CD-ROM), for which we thank them immensely. For teachers visiting Middle Earth to join us in the research project, please look out for Nimue, Thanatos and Elrond (their respective screen names) and join us in expressing appreciation to them for their work.

We would also like to thank the teachers whose exciting classroom work is showcased in Chapter 5. We are delighted to present their work as exemplary cases of teachers who are enhancing their classroom work in children's literature by the meaningful integration of ICT. These teachers include Mark Pearce, from Sydney, Australia, and Coco Veillette from Quebec, Canada. We are most grateful for their contributions to our work in this area. In Chapter 5 we have also mentioned the contributions of undergraduate students who designed lesson plans for the class working on an e-book. We wish to thank the University of Sydney BEd primary students who volunteered for the ELLIE project and made a contribution to the classroom lessons described in Chapter 5. In particular, we thank Lillian Wassef and Suzanne Teulan.

In Chapter 4 we discuss the work of Swiss educator Edgar Goetschi, who was kind enough to take us on a tour of his educational palace, *Meetpoint*, and to take time to explain how he used his palace in the classroom to teach foreign languages. We thank him for his time.

The authors would also like to acknowledge the graphic artists who designed original artwork for the room backgrounds of the *Kids, Enfants,*

Kinder palace. These are featured in Chapters 4 and 5. These talented artists include: Maarten Toner, Dan Backus and David Washington.

Our appreciation is also extended to the following people for giving us permission to reprint their images: Roger Garland (for his Tolkien-inspired artwork illustrated in Chapter 6), and Scott Martins, of Worlds Apart Productions, for allowing us to print a screenshot of the role-playing MUD featured in Chapter 4. We would also like to thank Lothian Books for permission to reproduce the cover and two pages from *Dreamwalker* by Isobelle Carmody and Steve Woolman.

Introduction

Children's literature continues to develop as a popular and enriching cultural and educational experience, and as a valued resource for literacy teaching in schools. More and more computer-based activities related to children's literature are now becoming available, but the evidence is that the majority of teachers, even younger, recent graduates, are in need of guidance in seeking to make effective use of the computer facilities that are now widely accessible in their schools and classrooms. At the same time, more and more children routinely use computers outside of school to access their interests. The burgeoning of children's literature sites on the internet reflects not only the popularity of children's books but also the integral part played by the internet in children's experience of such books. The popularity of the computer connection with children's literature is also reflected in the recent production of new CD-ROM versions of classic children's books such as *Alice's Adventures in Wonderland* and *The Little Prince* and popular contemporary stories such as *Stellaluna* and *The Polar Express*. Exciting new forms of digital narrative for children are also appearing in CD-ROM format and on the world wide web (www) and more and more children are communicating their experience of story via email, and various forms of electronic forums and chatrooms.

This book shows how the use of computers in English teaching can enhance and extend the engagement of computer-age children with the enchantment of the possible worlds of literary narratives. The focus is on the use of computer resources in teaching with conventional book-based literary texts. While the orientation is one of practical support for classroom teachers, it is 'research-led' support, reporting the results to date of a range of ongoing studies by the authors, dealing with the nature of image/text relations and their role in the construction of literary narratives, relationships between conventional book and computer-based versions of ostensibly the same literary narratives, and the role of on-line communities of various kinds in the critical appreciation of children's books and the interpretation and generation of new forms of multimodal, digital narratives. The teachers we have worked with have enthusiastically taken up the classroom implications of our research and have adopted an 'action-research' orientation, investigating optimal adaptations for meeting the needs of the particular classes of children they teach. Here we will introduce the theoretical and practical research bases for this teaching, provide examples of programmes of classroom work, and encourage our readers to explore the ideas in their own classrooms, seeking support and sharing experiences on our Electronic Literature and Literacies in International Education (ELLIE) website (http://sirius.linknet.com.au/ellie/).

The first chapter deals with the enduring and evolving nature of literature for children in a world in which conventional and digital multimedia routinely provide multiple versions of the same 'story' and where relationships among stories and explicit attention to the 'constructedness' of story are so much a part of the engagement of readers/viewers. In this chapter we outline 'usable' tools for classroom work on developing children's understanding of 'visual grammar' as a resource for interpreting and constructing images, and key concepts in a functional approach to verbal grammar as a means of understanding how language is deployed to achieve different kinds of meanings. It is this semiotic knowledge that will assist teachers to work with children on critically understanding the inter-relatedness of 'how' stories are constructed in both conventional and computer-based formats and 'what' the stories are telling them.

Chapter 2 discusses well-known works of children's literature that have been re-published in CD-ROM format and on the worldwide web (www), and also the sources and types of on-line resources for working with published children's literature in book format. In comparing electronic and book versions of literary texts we make use of the functional approaches to visual and verbal grammar outlined in Chapter 1 and explore the commonalities and differences in the interpretive possibilities of the different story versions. As well as listing many useful websites for enhancing work with particular books and authors, we also provide a framework for describing the aspects of work with literature that the on-line materials support. These include the context of composition, dealing with author background, story sources, unpublished drafts and related stories; the context of interaction, dealing with the materially interactive/agentive role of the reader, the blurring of story comprehension and composition, hypertext and non-linear reading, and 'search/ selective' reading of story; and the context of response, concerned with reader–author and reader–reader interaction via email, chatrooms, on-line comprehension and reading extension activities. Finally, in this chapter, we exemplify various types of on-line resources for working with an illustrated novel for young adolescents – *Dreamwalker* by Isobelle Carmody and Steven Woolman (2001), indicating www sites available to support teaching/learning activities for this book as well as complementary off-line work.

Chapter 3 is an introduction to 'book raps'. Essentially a book rap is a conversation about reading a book that takes place on-line among school children over a number of weeks. In this chapter we propose participation in book raps as a useful addition to within-class discussion of books. We explain how teachers can organize for their classes to participate in book raps and indicate a range of websites that conduct raps. Illustrative evidence for the benefits of book raps to student learning is included as is a sample unit of work showing how participation in a book rap can be incorporated into the regular classroom teaching programme. Teachers and their students can participate in book raps at different levels of involvement from passive observation to the generation of new raps. Book raps are also one area where the application of ICT to classroom learning can be achieved without requiring teachers to have high levels of technological expertise.

Chapter 4 explains two different types of on-line communities or 'virtual worlds': a MUD (multi-user domain or multi-user dungeon) and a palace. A very large number of these virtual worlds exist in cyberspace. People of all ages join these worlds for the enjoyment of interaction with the communities. Many virtual worlds involve intensive role-playing as a means of constructing a collaborative narrative. Participants communicate through a wide range of literate practices from spoken text, to computer commands, to visual images, to the use of sound effects or sound bytes. We describe how these virtual worlds operate and provide examples and discussions of the types of collaborative literary narratives in which children can participate on-line. One of these is a MUD called 'Moose Crossing', which was designed by children for children, and another is a palace called 'Kids, Enfants, Kinder'. In each case we detail the multiliteracies (Unsworth, 2001) children are learning through their participation and we also show how these virtual worlds can enhance classroom work with children's literature and literacy.

In Chapter 5 we illustrate the work of three teachers: Jenny, Mark and Coco, who have gradually been integrating the use of computers into their classroom practices. The snapshot of Jenny's classroom illustrates a teacher beginning to include websites to enrich literature-based units of work that have a focus on visual literacy and narrative structures, putting into practice some of the ideas outlined in Chapters 1 and 2. Her unit of work described in this chapter is designed for younger children aged 7 to 9. The snapshot of Mark's classroom reflects his efforts to engage his class, in which many of the children have English as a second language, in interactions with children from Finland. He worked with the authors on a project called ELLIE (Electronic Literature and Literacies in International Education) to explore the use of electronic forums (similar to the book raps described in Chapter 3) to excite and stimulate children's discussions about novels and e-books. Coco's snapshot represents a teacher with an interest in developing her children's collaborative narrative writing using the on-line virtual environment of the palace, as discussed in Chapter 4.

In the final chapter, we invite teachers to undertake a programme of work with their own students, which adopts the transformative classroom literacy practices we have described in the previous chapters. We suggest an action research approach investigating the impact of the changes on student learning as part of the normal classroom teaching/learning programme. To this end we outline a research plan and provide the tools to begin the work. We offer a programme of lesson plans, teaching strategies and methods of observing and analyzing what children are doing with children's literature and ICT, focusing on the world of Tolkien: Middle Earth. The main site for classroom work and associated action research will be the Middle Earth palace (Sorenson, 2000–2004, on-line), a g-rated visual virtual world. We also offer a means of sharing classroom experiences and communicating the research outcomes, through publication on the ELLIE website.

Our aim is to collect teachers' reports about the research to share with others, and to develop a network of educators who are willing to trial and explore the most effective means of developing children's multiliteracies in digital contexts. We hope that this book will help introduce more computer-based activities related to children's literature into primary classrooms.

1 Changing dimensions of children's literature

Introduction

Many children today are well oriented to engaging with the 'radical change' in narrative form and presentation of contemporary children's literature (Dresang, 1999) because their out-of-school experience with fictional narrative characters often embraces their various incarnations in picture books, cartoons, videos, DVDs and CDs, as well as in traditional and electronic games. While children's out-of-school experience of fictional narrative may 'tune' them to much of the innovative narrative form and technique of contemporary picture books and novels (as well as accompanying multimedia 'backstories' and para texts), this is frequently not the case for their teachers (and their parents). Nevertheless, children's literature continues to be seen as a crucial resource in nurturing the child's progress from basic literacy to a level of critical and cultural literacy necessary for effective adult life (Hollindale, 1995). As Margaret Meek has long pointed out, it is the kinds of texts that children have access to and the kinds of interactions they experience around those texts that influence the kinds of readers they become (Meek, 1988). To sustain the facilitative role of children's literature in classroom literacy development we need to understand the evolving nature of children's books as objects in their own right and also how they are positioned by publishers, educators and readers as phenomena in the new multimedia world in which so many children move so easily.

In this chapter we will focus on children's books as objects in their own right. First, we will indicate some of the key aspects of 'radical change' that characterize current and emerging literary texts for children. Second, we will outline recent work on a 'grammar of visual design' (Kress and van Leeuwen, 1996), which provides an accessible and systematic description of the meaning-making resources of images and helps us to understand the changing narrative role of images in children's literature. Third, we will show how functional descriptions of verbal grammar (Halliday, 1994; Matthiessen, 1995) can provide both an accessible interpretive resource for teachers and children working with the text of literary narrative and a common theoretical basis with the functional grammar of images, facilitating understanding of image–text interaction in meaning-making. In Chapter 2 we will take up the positioning of children's literature in the multimedia world, the contextualization of children's books on the internet and the recontextualization of some literary texts in electronic format on CD-ROMs and on the worldwide web.

Radical change in children's literature in a screen-age culture

Children growing up in the early years of the twenty-first century have been born into a culture that differs immeasurably from past cultures. These children are the 'net-generation' who take the personal computer and the internet for granted. Communication in this digital culture is marked by the interactivity, immediacy, and complexity of both images and text. This is a culture that has facilitated and promoted the 'radical change' in books for children in a way that has never been done before (Dresang, 1999). The construct of radical change was developed by Dresang (1999) to identify and explain books with characteristics reflecting the interactivity, connectivity and access that characterize our emerging digital society. Some books with these characteristics predate contemporary digital culture as noted by Dresang and by Mackey (1994), but for the net-generation, semiotic devices such as cuts, flashbacks, split-screen images, hyperlinks and non-linear progression, multiple conclusions, etc., are very much the norm. Increasingly, these devices are deployed in ways that integrate the use of language and image. In a textual habitat saturated with images, moving and still, alone and in all manner of hybrid combinations with texts and sounds, today's children are likely to possess a richer and more acute understanding of visual imagery and its modes of deployment than any other generation (Lewis, 2001). Children's literature is a key source of sustained reading by net-generation students, but to optimize its potential for learning, teachers need to appreciate the nature of the radical change in these books, which engage young readers.

Three categories of radical change are identified by Dresang: (1) changing forms and formats; (2) changing perspectives; and (3) changing boundaries. In the latter category, Dresang discusses the complex ways in which characters are presented and the greater frequency of 'unsolved endings' as well as the representation of new communities and treatment of previously 'forbidden' topics. The focus here will be more on the first two of Dresang's categories, dealing with aspects of narrative technique.

Changing forms and formats

David Macaulay's (1990) *Black and White* is cited by Dresang as exemplifying in its narrative technique the non-linearity of hypertext. It consists of inter-related storylines involving parents and their children, a herd of cows, a train journey, and an escaped convict. All four storylines are represented on each double-page spread, each illustrated with a distinctive style and palette and each with some connections woven into the others. Towards the end of the book, the four storylines break through their borders and come together, but the reader is left to speculate on the uncertainty of what happens next.

The Stinky Cheese Man and Other Fairly Stupid Tales (Scieszka and Smith, 1992) is metafictive work in that it explicitly draws attention in the text to its status as a constructed piece of fiction. In this story two narrators, Jack (of the beanstalk) and the Little Red Hen, interrupt the story and each other, present-ing an ironic and non-linear narrative where words become pictures, and the pictures not only illustrate the content but also the playful disruptions to the narrative. David Wiesner's *The Three Pigs* (Wiesner, 2001) is also a metafictive tale. The wolf's huffing and puffing blows the first pig right out of the story. One by one, the pigs exit the story frame and follow their own adventures. After folding a page of their own story into a paper plane, they fly off to visit other storybooks. Again, variation in illustrative style and fonts and shifts in perspective are used to provoke readers to ponder the conventions of story as they engage with an unconventional story form.

Not all books reflecting the non-linear organization and format of digital media are picture books. Similar innovative formats occur in novels for young readers such as *Spring-Heeled Jack* by Philip Pullman (1989), which is fragmented, with multimodal pages, and quirky organization (Bearne, 2000). Other examples of novels using the non-linear organization characteristic of hypertext cited by Dresang are *Whirligig* (Fleischman, 1998) and *Holes* (Sacher, 1998).

Changing perspectives

The construction of story from a singular point of view via a distanced omniscient narrator has given way to some extent in contemporary fiction to more frequent inclusion of multiple points of view often voiced by characters who 'speak for themselves', or by a narrator who adopts variable points of view throughout the story. These have been referred to as polyphonic narratives (McCallum, 1999). Dresang (1999) cites recent examples of polyphonic narra-tives. For example, *Making up Megaboy* (Walter, 1998) is the story of an 'average kid', Robbie Jones, who, on his thirteenth birthday, shoots a Korean shop-keeper. The story is told in short media-like accounts and computer-generated graphic representations of 19 people associated with Robbie – his parents, friends, minister, teacher, a lawyer, a news anchor-person, the barber and others. Robbie never speaks for himself. The story raises questions about how such a thing could happen and the community in which the boy lived could not imagine why he would do it. But shifts in point of view also occur in more light-hearted stories such as 'Unhappily Ever After' in the collection *Quirky Tales* by Paul Jennings (1987). In this story, a young boy, Albert, is about to receive corporal punishment from his balding old headmaster for allegedly circulating a note ('BALD HEAD BROWN WENT TO TOWN RIDING ON A PONY'). The story begins from Albert's point of view:

> Albert pulled up his socks and wiped his sweaty hands on the seat of his pants. He did up the top button of his shirt and adjusted his school tie. Then he trudged slowly up the stairs.
>
> He was going to get the strap.
>
> He knew it, he just knew it. He couldn't think of one thing he had done wrong but he knew Mr Brown was going to give him the strap anyway. He would find some excuse to whack Albert – he always did.

Then there is a shift to Mr Brown's point of view as Albert knocks on Mr Brown's door:

> Inside the room Brown heard the knock. He said nothing. Let the little beggar suffer. Let the little smart alec think he was in luck. Let him think no one was in.
>
> Brown heard Albert's soft footsteps going away from the door. 'Come in, Jenkins,' he boomed.

Such changing perspectives are also a feature of contemporary picture books where both language and images are used to construct different points of view. Anthony Browne's *Voices in the Park* (Browne, 1998) constructs the 'same' event of a visit to the park from the point of view of a mother, her son and a father and his daughter. Not only is the representation of the event quite different in each case, but also the appearance of the park changes according to the perspective of the character from whose point of view the event is communicated.

The role of images in the construction of complex variation in point of view in picture books has been demonstrated by Williams (1998) in his discussion of images in Anthony Browne's *Gorilla* (Browne, 1983). Williams notes the association of changes in vertical angle with variation in point of view. Initially the high angle views of Hannah position the reader as more powerful in observing 'just a little child'. However, when Hannah makes a request of her father in the fourth image, the reader takes up a vertical angle, which is much lower and is, in fact, an exaggeration of Hannah's perspective. 'The reader is no longer positioned as just an observer of the girl, but literally associated with her perspective by taking on a similar power position with respect to the father' (Williams, 1998: 29). Williams goes on to point out that there is no stable relationship with respect to power between the reader and the focalizing character, so the child reader cannot simply associate with Hannah's orientation, at least not in any simple sense of identification. Williams sees this aspect of the visual construction of point of view as most important for discussion of children's entry into visual practices in that young readers are simultaneously positioned as both engaged as part of the narrativized experience and somewhat detached from it as observer of Hannah's actions and responses.

The kind of image analyses in Williams' work with *Gorilla* has also been useful in explicating changes in point of view that occur when picture books are recontextualized in multimedia CD-ROM formats. *Stellaluna* (Cannon, 1996) is constructed from quite different points of view in the book and electronic versions (Unsworth, 2003b) and the animated images in the CD-ROM version of *The Little Prince* (de Saint-Exupéry, 2000) also construct different points of view from those in the linear and book versions (Unsworth, 2003a). In the next section we will explain this kind of image analysis and further indicate its usefulness in working with children's literature.

Re-thinking reading images in picture books: a 'grammar of visual design'

The interactivity of contemporary literature for children constructs young readers as active meaning-makers 'filling in' the possibilities left by interpretive 'gaps' or ambiguities within the text, images or the interaction between them (Lonsdale, 1993; Meek, 1988; Prain, 1998; Stephens and Watson, 1994; K. Watson, 1997; Williams, 1987). But the extent to which such active interpretive reading is taken up is also influenced by the kinds of shared talk children experience about texts. Teachers, parents and other co-readers who appreciate the interactive complexity of children's books and can enjoy with children both the story and the visual and verbal means by which it is constructed, not only encourage pleasure in reading, but also enhance 'net-age' children's analytic satisfaction of understanding the ways in which the text is producing pleasure and how it is positioning them as interpretive agents (Chambers, 1985; Meek, 1988; Misson, 1998). In order to facilitate such interactions, this section of the chapter addresses the role of explicit, systematic knowledge about the meaning-making resources of images.

Far from lessening children's enjoyment of literature, analyzing the means by which images make meanings helps them feel they are getting closer to the texts and what it is they enjoy about them (Misson, 1998: 108; Nodelman,

1988: 37). However, if children are to learn how to analyze the ways images make meanings, they need to gain knowledge of the visual meaning-making systems deployed in images. There is significant support for the view that systematic knowledge of this kind is essential and that it should be explicitly taught (Doonan, 1993: 8; Nodelman, 1988: 37). But what kind of description of visual meaning-making resources is most appropriate for analyzing multimodal literary texts for children? The grammar of visual design described by Gunther Kress and Thao van Leeuwen has been shown to be a productive analytic resource in recent work with children's literature (Astorga, 1999; Lewis, 2001; Stephens, 2000; Styles and Arizpe, 2001; Unsworth, 2001, 2003b; Williams, 1998, 2000), which can be used in explicit teaching with young children (Callow and Zammit, 2002).

Kress and van Leeuwen's work (1996, 2001) recognizes that images, like language, realize not only representations of *material reality* but also the interpersonal interaction of *social reality* (such as relations between viewers and what is viewed). The work also recognizes that images cohere into textual compositions in different ways and thus realize *semiotic reality*. More technically, Kress and van Leeuwen's functional semiotic account of images adopts from systemic functional linguistics the metafunctional organization of meaning-making resources:

- the ideational metafunction involves the representation of objects and their relations in the material world;
- the interpersonal metafunction involves the nature of the relationships among the interactive participants;
- the textual metafunction deals with the ways in which linguistic and/ or visual signs can cohere to form texts.

Here we will explore ways in which this metafunctional framework adopted by Kress and van Leeuwen can describe visual meaning-making in picture books. Although, as in language, the three metafunctions are realized simultaneously, we will initially discuss each separately. First, we will consider aspects of *representational* structures, which visually construct the nature of events, the objects and participants involved, and the circumstances in which they occur. Secondly, we will examine the construction of *interactive* meanings in images, which include the interpersonal relationship between the viewer and the represented participants. Then we will investigate how aspects of layout construct *compositional* meanings, which are concerned with the distribution of the information value or relative emphasis among elements of the image. As far as possible we will draw examples of images from one book, *Zoo*, by Anthony Browne, but where necessary we will also refer to other well-known picture books.

Representational meanings

According to Kress and van Leeuwen, images construct representations of reality that are either 'narrative' or 'conceptual'. Narrative images can depict participants (human or non-human) participating in actional, reactional, verbal events or mental events (the latter by means of 'thought clouds'). Sometimes several of these processes occur in the same image. Representational images are characterized by the presence of 'action lines' or 'vectors' and/or speech balloons and thought clouds. Action lines can be seen in *Zoo* in the fourth image in the book showing the family walking along a path and 'Harry' climbing a pole. For example, with Dad and the older son the vectors formed by the right leg advanced and the heel of the left leg lifted from the ground generate the vectors we read conventionally as indicating walking forward. This image also illustrates verbal processes showing the mouths of Mum and Dad slightly open and speech balloons containing their utterances. The walking processes in this image are actional because the participants are not acting upon anyone or anything else. However, such processes can be 'transactional' if the participant is acting on someone or something else, as is the case with the boys wrestling each other in the image opposite the rhinoceros.

Reactional processes are when the participant's eyeline is directed to another participant. In *Zoo*, opposite the image of the orang-utan is a crowd image in which all participants are reacting to something. In the case of Mum in this image, this is noticeable because her head and body are slightly tilted, indicating her close observation in reaction to something. Reactional processes like these are non-transactional because the phenomenon the participant is reacting to is not shown within the image. Such images are an important narrative technique in creating the 'gaps' to be filled by the active reader. In this case we infer the people in the crowd are reacting to the orang-utan, but because the gaze of Mum and a number of other participants is directly towards us, we are positioned with the point of view of the zoo animals. The types of processes in which characters participate in images are important in characterization and to the ways in which particular points of view are privileged by the author/illustrator. In *Zoo*, Mum appears in only four images. Three of these depict her in non-transactional reactional processes, such as the one we have described, and in all cases she appears to be looking directly at us. The last of these images is aligned with Mum's utterance towards the end of the book:

"I don't think the zoo really is for animals," said Mum.

Reactional processes can be transactional where both the reacting participant and the phenomenon appear in the same image. There are no such images in *Zoo*. In *Gorilla* (Browne, 1983), however, there are several such images. One of note is the triptych showing the toy gorilla and the doll where the gorilla grows in size over the three images. The final image in the triptych shows the startled doll with hair standing on end looking at the enormous gorilla.

There are also no examples of thought clouds in *Zoo*. In Pat Hutchins' *Don't Forget the Bacon* (Hutchins, 1978), we find both speech bubbles and thought clouds, with the latter being central to the way the book plays with the strategy of mental rehearsing of the shopping list in order to remember all the items. Conceptual images depict classifications or part–whole relations or symbolic relations. In *Zoo*, the first image showing separate images of the four members of the family arranged in tabular format under the heading 'My Family' is an example of such a conceptual classificatory image. Further examples of this kind of conceptual classificatory image occur in *Piggybook* (Browne, 1986), where we have the double-page spread of four images depicting the various kinds of work done by Mum during the day and a subsequent page of four images showing the work she did at night. While such conceptual images are not common in picture books, conceptual symbolic images occur very frequently. In *Zoo*, there is the obvious symbolic image of Dad with the clouds in the shape of horns positioned on each side of his head, as well as many more complex symbolic attributes in images such as the symbolic crucifixion in the close-up image of the gorilla (Styles and Arizpe, 2001).

While the actional, reactional, mental and verbal processes in which participants are involved are the central aspects of the visual narrative structures described by Kress and van Leeuwen, they occur in circumstances such as the *setting* in which the processes take place, the *means* by which the processes are effected and the *accompaniment* of other participants while such processes take place. Far from being an inert background, the settings of images can provoke active engagement of the reader in the nature of the development of the narrative. This can be easily seen in the provocative aspects of the settings of the images in *Zoo*. For example, the pattern of grass in the setting for the image of the tiger, implying the mirror shape of a tiger and further implying the tiger's constant pacing backwards and forwards. Circumstances of means, dealing with the instruments by which processes are effected can be equally intriguingly provocative. For instance, the second image in *Where the Wild Things Are* (Sendak, 1962) shows Max chasing the dog. But why is Max chasing the dog with a fork? Circumstances of accompaniment in the images of picture books are often commented upon in the context of some readers failing to notice that minor participants accompanying the main participants are involved in their own subsidiary narrative in the sequence of images. In *Don't Forget the Bacon* (Hutchins, 1978), there is the dog being tantalized/tormented by the butterfly throughout the story and it has been reported (V. Watson, 1996: 151) that adult readers frequently do not notice the adventurous baby in *Chicken Licken* (Ormerod, 1985).

Interactive meanings

We will outline three main aspects of the account of interactive meaning in images provided by Kress and van Leeuwen (1996). The first of these is the kind of contact between the viewer and the represented participants in the image – whether the viewer interpersonally interacts with or observes the represented participants. The second aspect is the social distance – whether the image is located along a continuum characterized by a close-up, medium or long shot. The third aspect is the interpersonal attitude that is constructed by the vertical angle (high, medium or low shot) and the horizontal angle (whether the representation is from an oblique angle or whether the viewer seems to be parallel or 'front on' to the image).

One kind of contact between a viewer and the represented participants is referred to by Kress and van Leeuwen as a 'demand'. This is where the gaze of one or more of the represented participants is directly towards the viewer. As we have already mentioned, three of the four images in which Mum is depicted in *Zoo* are demands, with Mum's gaze directly toward us as viewers. The image of Dad with the clouds positioned to imply horns on the side of his head is also a demand with Dad looking directly at us. Such images engage the viewer in a kind of direct pseudo-social interpersonal exchange with the participant(s) in the image. These images occur less frequently in picture books than those which do not engage the viewer in this way (Nodelman, 1988: 151). Images in which there is no direct gaze toward the viewer are called 'offers' by Kress and van Leeuwen. In *Zoo*, all the images of the animals are offers. None of the animals, including the close-up image of the gorilla, have their eyeline oriented directly to the viewer (cf. Styles and Arizpe, 2001).

The social distance in the early pages of *Zoo* is quite remote with fairly long shots depicting the family as they drive to the zoo and somewhat distant as they line up for their tickets. The image of the boys wrestling is more of a medium social distance, where although we can see all of their bodies, they are bent over and as such fill the frame, so we appear quite close to them. The image of Dad with the cloud-horns is much closer and the image of him laughing is a fairly intimate close-up. We have noted that most of the images of Mum are demands and, in fact, the first of these is a medium to close-up image with the rest more distant, perhaps to intensify the viewer/participant interaction and alignment of the viewer with the point of view that Mum represents both in this image and in the subsequent ones. Most of the animal images are socially quite remote, with one or two approaching medium social distance such as the orang-utan and the tiger. The striking exception to this pattern is the extremely intimate close-up of the gorilla.

The vertical angle of the image accords relative power to the viewer or the represented participant(s). Low-angle images show the represented participants looking down on the viewer and hence the represented participant is accorded more power the lower this vertical angle is. This is used to great effect in *Zoo* with the cloud-horned image of Dad represented as towering over the positioning of the viewer, indicative of the power Dad exercises in the family. A noteworthy high-angle image is that of the orang-utan ('Miserable thing') emphasizing its 'downtrodden' demeanour and lack of power. It is also interesting that the first demand image of Mum looking through the green grille wire is at eye level with the viewer, indicating equality of power.

When the viewer is 'front on' or the horizontal angle of the image is parallel, the effect is to maximize the viewer's involvement or identification with the world of the represented participants. In *Zoo*, once the family is inside, the majority of the images depicting them have parallel horizontal angles maximizing our involvement with them. This is not the case for the depiction of the animals. Our view of them is side on or from an oblique angle. Even with the close-up of the gorilla, the frontal angle is not parallel. We are probably closest to being 'front on' with the baboons, and Mum's comment is interesting here:

> "They remind me of someone," said Mum. "I can't think who."

One further aspect of interactive meaning described by Kress and van Leeuwen is modality. This refers to the extent to which an image depicts the realism of the aspects of the world it represents and is determined by the benchmark of the high quality colour photograph. People judge an image to be 'naturalistic' if it approximates this level of representation. Colour is a major influence on naturalistic modality. Naturalistic images have high colour saturation rather than black and white. Their colours are diversified rather than monochrome, and they are modulated, using many shades of the various colours. Modality also varies along a scale from maximum delineation of detail features of parti-cipants to the schematization of detail. In highly schematic images a head may be represented by a circle, the eyes by two dots, and the mouth by a curved line. In *Zoo*, the family is depicted with somewhat lower modality than the animals and within the animals the highest modality occurs in the close-up of the gorilla. Lower modality tends to imply more generic representation and perhaps in *Zoo* this helps to generalize the attitudes portrayed by the family. The high modality of the gorilla combines with the extreme close-up to effect the intimacy of the interaction with the viewer.

Compositional meanings

In picture books the double-page spread is the usual syntagm with left/right division the most common means of organizing the information value of the images. This reflects the feature of written English where what is given infor-mation occurs in the first part of the clause and what is new comes at the end of the clause (Halliday, 1994: 296–302). In John Burningham's *Come Away from the Water, Shirley* (Burningham, 1977), the given situation of the parents commanding Shirley from their seats on the beach always occurs on the left-hand page and the new situations of Shirley's adventure are always depicted on the right. On the other hand, somewhat unusually in Burningham's *Granpa* (Burningham, 1984), it is the imagined or remembered situation that is consistently depicted on the left and the given or familiar situation on the right. In Anthony Browne's *Zoo*, once the family have arrived at the zoo, the humans are consistently on the left and the animals on the right.

The form of framing of images, or lack thereof, is a very active feature of layout in constructing the nature of the narrative. In *Zoo*, the framing around the images of the family is not prominent nor straight – as if the images had been cut out from somewhere else. By contrast, once the family arrive at the zoo, the images of the zoo animals are all on the right-hand pages and they are all heavily framed with thick, black, straight border lines. This pattern is maintained until we see a much more distinct albeit not quite straight grey-black bordering around the image of the boys wearing their monkey hats. Then we see a distinct yellow border around the image of the family and other members of the public looking at the orang-utan. Then the second last image of the book shows the older son, the narrator, who had a very strange dream in his room that night. This image has the same thick, black, straight border that surrounded all of the images of the animals in the zoo, so the transposition of framing is complete. There is one exception to the framing style for the images of the zoo animals. This is in the image of the gorilla. Note that, from a naturalistic point of view, this is the image of highest modality in the book and it is at a very intimate social distance. The gaps in the outside border separating the quadrants mean that the gorilla's face is actually divided into four separate pieces. We have earlier noted the crucifixion symbolism of this image. Suffice it to say that the use of framing is far from incidental to the construction of the interpretive possibilities of this book.

Even this brief outline of key elements in Kress and van Leeuwen's grammar of visual design indicates the ways in which knowledge about the visual resources for constructing the different kinds of meanings in images can enhance the opportunities for learning in talk around texts and increase the potential for expanding young readers' interpretive reading practices.

Re-thinking interpretive reading: engaging with the grammatical form of literary texts

If we are to help children understand some of the ways in which literary texts achieve their effects, we need to have access to the kind of grammatical description that will enable us to talk directly about language form and its use in constructing the various kinds of meanings at stake. Systemic functional grammar (SFG) provides the kind of resource that teachers, and ultimately children (Williams, 1998, 2000), can use to enhance their understanding of the relationship between the 'what' and the 'how' of literary texts. Space will not permit a detailed account of SFG for these purposes here – for an accessible, chapter-length introduction to basic concepts of functional grammar, see Ravelli (2000), Unsworth (2001) and Williams (1993) – however, we can gain an appreciation of the use of key functional grammatical concepts as interpretive resources by applying them to a 'grammatical' reading of Anthony Browne's *Zoo*.

SFG proposes that all clauses in all texts simultaneously construct three types of meanings. These are the same three types of meanings described earlier as the basis for Kress and van Leeuwen's grammar of visual design:

- ideational meanings involve the representation of objects, events and the circumstances of their relations in the material world;
- interpersonal meanings involve the nature of the relationships among the interactive participants;
- textual meanings deal with the ways in which linguistic signs can cohere to form texts.

Ideational meanings are realized grammatically by Participants, Processes and Circumstances of various kinds. Circumstances correspond to what is traditionally known as adverbs and adverbial phrases. Processes correspond to the verbal group, but Processes are semantically differentiated. Material Processes, for example, express actions or events (like 'walk', 'sit' or 'travel'), while Mental Processes deal with thinking, feeling and perceiving ('understand', 'detest', 'see') and Verbal Processes deal with saying of various kinds ('demand', 'shout', 'plead'). These different kinds of Processes have their own specific categories of participants. Material Processes, for example, entail Actors (those initiating the process) and Goals (those to whom the action is directed), while Mental Processes entail a Sensor and a Phenomenon.

Interpersonal meanings are realized by the mood and modality systems. Much of this aspect of functional grammar is familiar to those with experience of more traditional grammars. The declarative, for example, is realized by the ordering of Subject followed by the Finite Verb, while the interrogative is realized by the inversion of this ordering. The modal verbs ('can', 'should', 'must', etc.) indicate degrees of obligation or inclination and modal adverbs like 'frequently', 'probably', 'certainly' enable personal stance to be communicated through negotiating the semantic space between 'yes' and 'no'.

Textual meanings are realized in part by the Theme/Rheme system. The Theme of a clause in functional grammar is that element that is in first position. This is usually the Subject ('<u>The weather</u> is mild in Australia'), but an adverbial element could be placed in Theme position ('<u>In Australia</u> the weather is mild'). This is not as common, and is likely to occur more frequently in more formal written language than in informal spoken language. When some ideational element other than the Subject is placed in first position in a clause, we call it a marked Theme, in that it draws more attention due to is relatively less frequent use.

Although the three major grammatical systems realize the three main types of meaning simultaneously, in order to show how they can be used as a resource for understanding the patterned construction of literary texts, the construction of ideational, interpersonal and textual meanings will be discussed separately in the following three sub-sections.

Textual meanings: Theme in *Zoo*

In *Zoo*, the Themes are mainly the family members or the animals and they are also the subject of the sentence so they are the most usual or 'unmarked' Theme choice:

> <u>Harry</u> started crying and <u>Dad</u> told me off.

> <u>Everyone</u> laughed except Mum, Harry and me.

> <u>The elephant</u> just stood in a corner stuffing its face.

The fact that marked Themes i.e. where, apart from conjunctive devices or modal adverbs like 'probably', etc., some other element like a complement or circumstantial adjunct (adverb or adverbial phrase) precedes the subject and is thus in the topical Theme position in the clause, occur much less frequently than unmarked Themes (where the subject precedes all other elements except conjunctives and modal adverbs) makes a marked Theme a signal that the reader's attention is being drawn to what is being dealt with at this point in the text. In some picture books marked Themes signal the episodic development of the story.

Marked Topical Themes occur in only five clauses in *Zoo* (Browne, 1994) and they are all located at the boundaries of episodes in the story as indicated in Table 1.1. In addition, in *Zoo* there is only one instance of a dependent clause preceding the main clause in a sentence:

> <u>When we finally got there</u> Dad *had* to have a row with the man in the ticket booth.

This can be understood as a clause functioning as a marked Theme (Martin, 1992: 435).

Table 1.1 Marked Themes reflect episodic boundaries in *Zoo*

Episode	Marked Themes
Orientation	<u>Last Sunday</u> we all went to the zoo.
In transit to the zoo	<u>After a while</u> Harry and I got really bored.
Events before lunch	<u>When we finally got there</u> Dad had to have a row with the man in the ticket booth.
Events after lunch	<u>After that</u> we went to the gift shop to spend our pocket money.
Conclusion	<u>In the car</u> Mum asked us what was the best bit of the day.
Coda	<u>That night</u> I had a very strange dream.

The role of the pattern of Theme selection in highlighting readers' perception of the structure of narrative and drawing attention to experiential meanings integral to interpretive possibilities of text segments has recently been discussed by Knowles and Malmkjaer (1996: 75) in relation to *The Secret Garden* (Burnett, 1992). They also discuss Thematization as 'a powerful tool for reinforcing a writer's explicit message'. To support this discussion they analyze part of the opening paragraph in the final chapter of *The Secret Garden* to point out how Burnett used Theme choice to pre-empt opposition to her strong claim about the effect of the mental lives of Mary and Colin on their physical condition.

Exploration of the patterning of Theme selection is an aspect of the analysis of textual meaning-making which can be introduced to very young readers to consider simple structural features of narrative. It can also introduce young readers to the ways in which writers draw attention to the interpretive possibilities of story and can be extended to the investigation of quite complex issues about the textual construction of ideological positioning in narratives. However, the textual meanings realized by Theme selection also need to be seen in a complementary relation to the realization of ideational and interpersonal meanings.

Ideational meanings: processes and participants in *Piggybook* and *Zoo*

In a study by Williams (1998) primary school children who had very little prior systematic knowledge of grammar were able to use functional descriptions of Process types, Participant and Circumstances, to see how different examples encode a variety of meanings relevant to the representation of character in Anthony Browne's *Piggybook* (Browne, 1986). The teacher drew attention to 'said' as the most common verb used in quoting or reporting speech and then experimented with the children in choosing alternative verbal processes like 'yelled', 'whispered', etc. It was this orientation and subsequent discrimination of verbal processes (saying verbs) that enabled the children to discuss the effect of Browne's selection of verbal processes like 'squealed', 'grunted', 'snorted' and 'snuffled'. The children were also able to appreciate that in the first part of the story Mrs Piggott was the only Actor engaged in Material Processes (action verbs) which entailed a Goal. While Mr Piggott and the boys were Actors in Material Processes, they didn't actually act upon anything whereas Mrs Piggott 'washed all the breakfast things . . . made all the beds . . . vacuumed all the carpets . . . and then she went to work'. At the end of the story, however, all the characters were Actors in Material Processes that had Goals, e.g. 'Patrick and Simon made the beds. Mr Piggott did the ironing.'

It is the introduction of the use of this metalanguage as a resource that facilitates further grammatically-based interpretive work. For example, in Anthony Browne's *Zoo*, Dad is the dominant Sayer (in 16 verbal processes), while Mum is the Sayer six times, as is the narrator, and Harry is the Sayer only once. But 'said' is only used three times to project/report Dad's speech. On the other occasions the Verbal Processes reporting/projecting Dad's speech are 'roared', 'snorted', 'howled', 'jeered', etc. However, for Mum and the narrator only 'said' is used. But beyond Verbal Processes, although the narrative is about an excursion, there is a fairly even distribution of Verbal, Material and Relational Processes, with Mental Processes being the least frequent. While the narrator and Harry are sometimes Senser in Mental Processes of perception ('Next we saw the baboons'), the only character who is Senser in Mental Processes of cognition is Mum – ('I don't think the zoo really is for animals'). As young readers are alerted to these patterns of grammatical choice, they can begin to read the 'constructedness' of characterization and the bases of alignments of readers with the point of view of particular characters.

Interpersonal meaning: mood and modality in *Zoo*

An examination of the deployment of the grammatical resources of the mood and modality systems in the dialogic text and the language of the narrator can also facilitate understanding of the construction of point of view and the differential alignment of readers with the various characters of the narrative. We will look first of all at the dialogic text in *Zoo*. Table 1.2 shows the distribution of speech functions.

Dad dominates the dialogue. He issues more commands and they are qualitatively different from Mum's commands. While Dad's commands are direct and at times intimidating ('Come DOWN you little ratbag!'), Mum's command is modified by the more positive vocative, 'boys', and by the inclusive imperative 'let's' (' "Come on, boys," said Mum, "let's get something to eat." ').

Dialogue is usually initiated by the questions from the boys or Dad. The

Table 1.2   Speech functions of characters in Anthony Browne's *Zoo*

Character	Total utterances	Command *Imperative*	Question *Interrogative*	Statement *Declarative*
Dad	14	3	4	7
Mum	7	2	0	5
Harry	4	1	1	2
I (narrator)	5	2	3	0

boys ask yes/no questions seeking permission (usually about eating) and why questions about their father's negative response to their earlier request. In contrast, the dialogue initiated by Dad is in the form of wh-questions which are riddle-type jokes and one rude rhetorical question about the boys ('Which one is the monkey?'). Although the boys are supposed to answer the riddles, the punchlines are actually supplied by Dad, which only he finds funny. So Dad does not engage in meaningful dialogue with the boys. Instead he either imposes his speech on them or answers their questions in the negative without giving reasons ('Because I say so.'). On the other hand, when Mum refuses the boys' request to have lunch, she does not do so with a direct 'no' but uses a declarative clause to express her negative answer. She says by way of explanation, 'But, we've only just got here.' The only time Dad addresses Mum directly is to refute her sympathetic utterance 'Poor thing', concerning the tiger.

Examining the interpersonal grammar of the dialogue, then, can contribute to an understanding of how character is constructed. But the mood and modality choices within the narration are also important in this respect. The use of modal verbs indicating a high level of obligation to describe Dad's behaviour points to the fact that Dad behaves this way habitually ('Dad had to have a row'; 'Dad had to do his King Kong impersonation'). The inclusion of mood adjuncts like 'sometimes' and 'of course' reinforces this notion of habitual behaviour ('Sometimes he can be really embarrassing'; 'Of course Dad had to do his King Kong impersonation'). And the comment adjunct 'luckily' indicates the feeling of relief in the narrator ('but luckily we were the only ones there'). The modal verbs and mood adjuncts also construct the narrator's judgments on events. For example, the unwelcome obligation to look at the polar bears and the boredom experienced in doing so is expressed not only by the negative attribute 'stupid' and repetition of the circumstance of location, 'up and down', but also in the high modal verb 'had to' and the modal adjunct 'just' ('Then we had to go and see the polar bear. It looked really stupid, just walking up and down, up and down.')

Conclusion

The use of these kinds of functional grammatical analyses and related image analyses has been shown to be viable, engaging and productive in classroom work with children (Callow and Zammit, 2002; Williams, 1998, 2000) and these have been incorporated in state education syllabus documents (Education Queensland, 1995; New South Wales Board of Studies, 1998). They have also been useful in explicating image/text relations in picture books, such as *The Rabbits* by John Marsden and Shaun Tan (Marsden and Tan, 1998), exemplifying aspects of Dresang's radical change (Unsworth and Wheeler, 2002). In Chapter 2 we will apply these analyses to explore the nature of the recontextualization of literary texts from book to various kinds of electronic presentation formats.

2 Exploring children's literature on CD-ROM and the www

Introduction

In this chapter we will investigate children's literature re-published in CD-ROM format and on the world wide web (www). We will also look at sources and types of on-line resources for working with published children's literature. Finally, we will discuss one example of an illustrated novel for young adolescents – *Dreamwalker* by Isobelle Carmody and Steven Woolman (2001). We will indicate a range of www resources available to support teaching/learning activities for this book and we will also outline the kind of complementary off-line work needed to develop children's knowledge about the verbal and visual grammatical construction of the interpretive possibilities of narrative.

CD-ROM versions of children's books

In this section we will consider the categories of children's literature produced on CD-ROMs, the media and presentation formats used, and the need for critical engagement with hypertext features as narrative techniques.

Types of children's literature on CD-ROM

The most commonly occurring categories of literature for children in CD-ROM format are traditional tales of various kinds, and what might be considered 'classic' children's stories – often originally published more than fifty years ago. Here we will not be concerned with purpose-written, instructional graded reading scheme stories such as those used in studies by Medwell (1998) and Lewin (2000). Stories like *The Three Pigs, Goldilocks and the Three Bears* and *Jack and the Beanstalk*, are now widely available in electronic format (see, for example, http://www.interactivebook.com), as are fables like *The Tortoise and the Hare* and other tales such as *The Golden Touch* (see, for example, http://www.antelope-ebooks.com). Quite a number of traditional tales published in book format in a variety of versions have been made into feature films and today many appear on DVDs as well as CD-ROM storybooks. A well-known recent example is the Disney movie and CD-ROM storybook of *Mulan* (Disney, 1998).

Classic books on CD-ROM include illustrated stories like those of Beatrix Potter such as *The Tale of Peter Rabbit* (Potter, 1987), Antoine de Saint-Exupéry's *The Little Prince* (de Saint-Exupéry, 2000), Lewis Carroll's *Alice's Adventures in Wonderland* (Carroll, 2000) and other children's novels like *The Secret Garden* (Burnett, 1992) and *Anne of Green Gables* (Montgomery, 1999). Relatively few contemporary literary texts for children are published in CD-ROM versions. Picture books currently regarded as works of children's literature rarely appear as CD-ROMs, with some notable exceptions such as *The Polar Express* (Van Allsburg, 1997), *The Paper Bag Princess* (Munsch, 1994), *Stellaluna* (Cannon, 1996), and *George Shrinks* (Joyce, c.1994). Similarly, it is usually only exceptional novels for children that subsequently appear as CD-ROMs, such as readings of the 'Harry Potter' books (Rowling, 1999) and innovative books like *Sophie's World* (Gaarder, c.1997).

Media and presentation format

Some books are re-published as audio CDs only, which may also include music background and various sound effects. On some CDs these audio features occur with the text and images. In some cases the images are static, simply transposed from page to screen. This is the case with *The Paper Bag Princess* (Munsch, 1994) for example. In other cases the original images from the book appear as animations on the CD as in *The Polar Express* (Van Allsburg, 1997). In this CD the animations activate automatically, but in others like *The Little Prince* (de Saint-Exupéry, 2000), the animations are controlled by the mouse 'clicks' of the viewer. This raises the issue of 'interactivity' as a key aspect of children's narrative experience in a digital age (Dresang and McClelland, 1999). Interactivity can relate to both 'navigation' through the digital text and story construction. Navigation concerns the selection of participation options such as having the story read to you or reading it yourself, and in the latter case then determining how to change to the next screen (usually 'turning the page' by clicking on the bottom right-hand corner), knowing how to 'quit' the story and return to it, and whether returning necessitates starting from the beginning or whether you can go directly to a particular page somewhere in the story. Such navigation matters are not completely separate from story construction since many CDs enable readers/viewers to choose particular parts of the story to read rather than proceeding linearly. As Margaret Mackey points out, given the structure and presentation of contemporary narratives and children's experience of electronic multimedia, 'It seems fairly clear that the idea of following the narrative thread from beginning to end of the story is now perceived very broadly as just one option for engaging with fiction' (1999: 28). A study of fifth grade children using CD-ROM stories indicated that few of the groups reading at the computer conformed to the convention of reading the text from start to finish (Trushell et al., 2001).

Interactivity also involves the construction of story from the presentation of print and images (as well as the audio). One aspect of this interactivity concerns the options for 'decoding' the text. On some CDs children may choose to have the text read aloud (often with highlighting of text segments synchronized with the voice over) or to read it themselves. The latter option may also allow children themselves to highlight text segments or single words and have just those read aloud. The other aspect of interactivity relating to story construction concerns the use of hypertext or 'hot spots' – frequently linked to elements in the images. Clicking on these activates some kind of animation and/or additional text, usually dialogue with audio. Such hot spots may be integral to the story, peripheral to the story or incongruous with the story. The CD-ROM version of *George Shrinks* (Joyce, c.1994) contains hot spots that are integral to the narrative. In this story George is left to look after the house and his younger sibling for a time while his parents are out. George literally shrinks to the size of a mouse and this turns the normal routines into a series of dramatic events fraught with danger as well as comedy, not the least of which concerns the now threatening company of the family cat. In the CD version the foreshadowing of the potential danger posed by the cat to the now very small George is achieved by clicking, which on one occasion activates the cat's paw reaching to the dressing table and towards the diminutive George in his bed. On the other hand the CD version of *Stellaluna* (Cannon, 1996) includes many incongruous hot spots with animated images which are gratuitous intrusions into the narrative. In this story a baby bat, Stellaluna, is separated from its mother when she was avoiding an attacking owl. Stellaluna lives in a nest with a family of young birds and adopts bird-like behaviours. Eventually Stellaluna and the mother bat are reunited but Stellaluna visits the birds she has made friends with and lived harmoniously with despite their differences. Clicking on images in the early part of the story initiates a number of activities of jungle animals which are quite unrelated to each other or to the story, like a monkey running up a tree, elephants splashing water at each other, a giraffe drinking and then gargling and a bird sliding down the giraffe's neck. In some CDs the hot spots are between these two extremes providing animations that are peripheral or incidental to the main concerns of the story. For example in *The Little Prince* (de Saint-Exupéry, 2000), clicking on his hand causes his sword to move or clicking on his shoulders causes his epaulettes to fly off and return to his shoulder. *The Little Prince* also contains many examples of hot spots that are integral to the narrative.

Developing a critical perspective on hypertext as a narrative device

Much of the research on hypertext in CD-ROM stories for children laments the role of incongruous hot spots distracting children from engagement with the actual story and the consequences for story recall and conventional measures of traditional story comprehension. Typically such researchers call for CD-ROM design that is more faithful to goals of engagement with story and character (Burrell and Trushell, 1997; Labbo and Reinking, 2000; Miller and Olsen, 1998; Trushell et al., 2001; Underwood, 2000). This seems eminently reasonable, but it does tend to maintain the orientation of the research (and teaching) to an exploration of new electronic routes to conventional literacy practices.

Literary authors and teachers may well seek to deploy hypertext resources towards the explication of plot theme and character, but as we have noted, the majority of CD-ROM narratives in children's literature are adaptations of traditional tales or classic stories. Given the social construction of these electronic books with multiple contributors to their composition and the demands of marketability, it is likely that hypertext will continue to be used for a range of 'product' engagement techniques. Some authors will become more familiar with hypertext and will co-opt it to generate innovative narrative techniques while, inevitably, in some texts what are seen as more frivolous uses of hot spots will continue. From a teaching point of view, it is important to 'harness' children's fascination with hypertext and develop their knowledge about various types and purposes, so that this kind of meta-knowledge can put them in a position to develop a critical appreciation of the use of hot spots. This may mean a more proactive focus both in teaching and research on hot spots that are integral to the thematic concerns of the story. Fortunately these are readily identified in a number of the more prolific and widely accessible CD-ROM stories. In one of the many 'Arthur' stories by Marc Brown, *Arthur's Teacher Trouble* (RandomHouse/Broderbund, 1994), which was used in the Underwood (2000) study, some hot spots were related to the storyline. For example, clicking on Arthur when he first meets his stern new teacher produced a 'thought cloud', which articulates Arthur's anxiety about being in this teacher's class. What is also needed is a more elaborated account of 'integral' and 'peripheral' hot spots to facilitate a more detailed understanding of the relationship between electronic presentational format and the interpretive practices of children reading these new digital narratives derived from the original book formats. It could be argued that reading the CD-ROM version of *George Shrinks* (Joyce, *c.*1994) or *The Little Prince* (de Saint-Exupéry, 2000) is in fact the experience of reading two quite different narratives from the book versions of those stories – with quite different interpretive practices and responses. This is largely due to the hypertext activations of different elements of the story and different points of view constructed through the hyperlinked animations (Unsworth, 2003).

WWW access to children's books

The longest-standing internet source of free books re-published on-line is Project Gutenberg (http://www.promo.net/pg/). It publishes books that are no longer in copyright, so these are books that were published before 1925. Many classics of children's literature such as the stories of Lewis Carroll, Sir Arthur Conan Doyle, Hans Christian Andersen, Edgar Allen Poe and Beatrix Potter are available. In general, these are available as 'text only' versions. The International Children's Digital Library (http://www.icdlbooks.org/) is a project of the University of Maryland and the internet Archive. It also provides free on-line versions of children's books which are out of copyright. For this collection the books are scanned and hence the original formats including illustrations are available on-line. Another resource is the University of Virginia's Electronic Text Centre (http://etext.lib.virginia.edu/subjects/Young-Readers.html). Again, out of copyright books have been scanned so that illustrations are included. The Rosetta project hosted by the University of Maryland (http://www.childrensbooksonline.org/) also provides scanned copies of classic and out of copyright children's books including illustrations. Other such collections are available at http://www.classicreader.com/, http://www.blackmask.com/page.php, http://www.bibliomania.com/, http://www.worldwideschool.org/library/ and http://www.fairrosa.info/. There are other sites with versions of classic stories that include text, animations and audio so that you can have the story read to you, or read it independently and typically also play an on-line game related to the story. One such site includes a number of the stories of Hans Christian Andersen (http://www.andersenfairytales.com/en/main).

As one would expect, very little current or relatively recently published literature for children is available on the web free of charge, as authors need to derive an income from their work. Nevertheless, from time to time some works are made available on-line by established authors. In 1995 Australian author, John Marsden, published a book entitled *Cool School: You Make it Happen* in the tradition of the 'choose your own adventure' stories. In this story the reader takes the part of a new student on the first day at a new school. A series of choices provides a variety of consequences which can make this a great day, or the worst ever. This story is currently available in its entirety as a 'webridged' hypertext story, which visitors can read on Marsden's website (http://www.panmacmillan.com.au/johnmarsden/csmain.htm – retrieved 4 April 2004). Popular Australian authors Paul Jennings and Morris Gleitzman regularly advertise offers of free (hardcopy) books to visitors to their websites. Their popular comic stories entitled *Wicked* were originally published as six separate volumes. These have now been re-published as single 'giant' volume (Jennings and Gleitzman, 1998), and Gleitzman is offering unsold copies of the second of the six originally separately published books (*Wicked Part 2*) as a 'giveaway' to visitors to his website who mail a request to him. As he notes, readers will be able to appreciate this story much better if they have read *Wicked Part 1*, so this is now available in full on his site (http://www.morrisgleitzman.com/ – retrieved 4 April 2004).

Using on-line resources for teaching with children's literature

There is a veritable plethora of websites that can be used to support teaching with children's literature. Here we will address strategies for identifying and then locating relevant sites, but more particularly we will outline a framework for clarifying the kinds of support for learning with children's literature that the various types of websites can provide.

To find sites at the point of teaching preparation need one can, of course, deploy a 'search engine' like yahoo or google and search on the book title and/ or author. This is likely to yield thousands of 'hits', which can then be refined by a more advanced search. However, it is useful to be aware of key categories of sites, which may enable more strategic 'surfing' to locate lesson support materials. Specialist sites dealing in detail with children's literature and education have become established over a number of years. Well regarded among these are the Carol Hurst site http://www.carolhurst.com/, the University of Calgary children's literature website http://www.acs.ucalgary.ca/~dkbrown/ and the Vandergrift's children's literature page hosted at Rutgers State University of New Jersey http://www.scils.rutgers.edu/~kvander/ChildrenLit/ index.html. These pages provide access to a wealth of information including links to author websites, resources for classroom learning activities, critical discussion of issues in children's literature, links to professional journals and associations and other websites related to children's literature. Publishers' websites are often a good starting point, especially for established authors and/or illustrators who tend to work with the one publishing company. They typically provide a link to or maintain the author's/illustrator's own website. A number of the sites listed have links related to 'visual literacy' and some specialist sites focus on the work of illustrators of children's literature, such as the site developed by the society of book illustrators in Australia (http:// www.thestylefile.com/about_us_page.htm). The International Board on Books for Young people (IBBY) (http://www.ibby.org/) and the Children's Book Council (http://www.cbcbooks.org/) provide an international perspective on children's literature, including awards and prizes for outstanding literary works for young readers.

When we look at websites to assist in implementing classroom work with children's literature, we find they provide, to varying degrees, material in one or more of five main categories:

1   The context of composition of the story.
2   The promotion of the book and enticement of potential readers.
3   Exploration/learning activities dealing with the construction of the story and its themes.
4   Opportunities for readers' response to the book.
5   Participation in book-related activities such as game-playing, purchase of book merchandising, etc.

The context of composition

This includes author/illustrator biographical information and often information about the genesis of the book. For example, if we go to Aidan Chambers' website: (http://www.aidanchambers.co.uk/), which we could locate by looking up 'authors' on the Penguin publishers site, or any one of the several children's literature sites we have mentioned, we will find some information on the genesis of *The Present Takers* (Chambers, 1983). Chambers says that a friend found out that his daughter was being badly bullied at school and that no one seemed to be able to stop it. The friend asked Aidan Chambers – as an ex-teacher – what he would do. Chambers says he didn't know what to say so he wrote the book to find an answer. He indicates that the first half of the story is pretty much the way it happened in real life and that he made up the second half. Similarly, David Almond (http://www.davidalmond.com/) comments on the origin of *Skellig* (Almond, 1998), explaining that the name comes from the Skellig Islands, which are off the south-west coast of Ireland. However, Almond says that he is not sure who or what the character Skellig is or where he comes from, how he got into the garage or where he goes to in the end. 'He remains a mystery – like much of life.'

The promotion of the book and enticement of potential readers

On publishers' and authors' websites this frequently includes excerpts from the book with audio to enable the potential reader to hear the story segment read aloud – sometimes by the author. David Almond on his website (http://www.davidalmond.com/) reads short excerpts from his novels. One chapter of each of Morris Gleitzman's books is available in text form on his site (http://www.morrisgleitzman.com/) and audio is available for several of these. As we noted, Gleitzman also offers hardcopy books as 'giveaways' and a similar offer is made from time to time by Paul Jennings http://www.pauljennings.com.au/. Readers may sample electronically one chapter from each of Beverly Cleary's books on-line (http://www.beverlycleary.com) and similar opportunities are available on many authors' and publishers' sites. On-line booksellers like Amazon.com (http://www.amazon.com) and Alibris (http://www.alibris.com) include short segments of the books with images (but not usually with audio). They also provide reviews including some sent by pur-chasers of the books.

Exploration/learning activities dealing with the construction of the book and its themes

These are sometimes provided on publishers' websites as well as on some of the other kinds of sites we have mentioned. The types of learning activities suggested vary widely. Some are fairly general ideas for classroom work. In common with most of the teaching suggestions provided on-line, the Beverly Cleary site (http://www.beverlycleary.com) offers classroom resources for all of the books as '.pdf' files that can be downloaded free of charge. The materials for the 'Ramona' books (Cleary, 1976, 1978, 1981, 1982, 1984, 1986) include summaries of the stories, character sketches of Ramona, her family, friends, teachers and other characters, and suggestions for classroom use of the books. The latter include 'read alouds', 'independent reading' and 'literature circles' and are very general suggestions such as:

> Arrange for four to six students to meet as a literature circle and dis-cuss books they have read about Ramona. Each literature circle could prepare a project based on its book(s) to present to the class.

Other suggested activities include responses to reading that are focused on activities outside the book rather than the narrative itself:

> When Ramona daydreams about having her mother all to herself in *Ramona and Her Mother*, she imagines her mother selecting books from her bookcase that she enjoyed hearing as a child. Using the descriptions Cleary provides throughout the various Ramona books, ask students to figure out what books might be in Ramona's bookcase. It might be fun to set up a Ramona bookcase in the classroom and invite students to read the books Ramona loves.

Lothian books (http://www.lothian.com.au) also provide 'downloadable' teaching resources for many books including *The Rabbits* (Marsden and Tan, 1998), which won the Children's Book Council Picturebook of the Year award in Australia in 1999. The book is a powerful allegory of colonization from the perspective of native Australian animals. It addresses the consequences of the arrival of a group of rabbits with a very different way of life. The rabbits bring new food and animals, and make their own houses to live in, eventually dominating the environment and its indigenous inhabitants. The publisher's website provides an extensive list of activities based on the book. What is clear, however, is that these are learning tasks to be undertaken and any actual teaching of the understandings required to respond to the tasks, for the most part, will have to be facilitated by the teacher, as can be seen in the following excerpt:

> **Activities**
>
> - Comment on the style of illustrations.
> - Read the book. Jot down some words to indicate what you felt after an initial reading. What words come to mind?
> - What is an allegory? A dictionary definition will give you an answer. Find other allegories – see if you can find some in picture book format.
> - This book is clearly not about rabbits. What do you think it is about? Why do you think *The Rabbits* was chosen as the title of the book? Give reasons for your answer. How are they depicted?
> - There is a paucity of words in this book, yet they are used with tremendous effect. Find examples where words are used unusually to convey a concept. Explain what effect those words have.
>
> (retrieved from http://www.lothian.com.au, 16 May 2004)

Our current research into the web-based pedagogic resources for working with children's literature (Olondriz Ortigas and Unsworth, forthcoming) suggests that teachers can contribute a great deal to enhance currently available material. What is needed is more emphasis on learning experiences providing explicit guidance to assist children in appreciating the narrative art of literary texts through an understanding of the grammatical choices of image and language that construct the engaging interpretive possibilities of the story. Part of our data concerning websites using the picture books of David Wiesner demonstrates our viewpoint.

The extent and range of websites dealing with Wiesner's books (all retrieved on or about 1 October 2003) indicate they are a popular tool for learning and that they are used by classroom teachers in a variety of ways. It seems that the majority of web-lessons involving Wiesner's books focus mainly on two types of activities. The first type uses the book as a starting point for broader thematic units. For instance, *Tuesday* (Wiesner, 1991) is read to begin a study of the use of transition words to show that time has elapsed. The class is then asked to use these words to write about the life cycle of a plant or animal (http://www.tie-online.org/2002/handouts2000/lessons.pdf-). A sample *Sector 7* (Wiesner, 1999) activity asks students to use cotton balls, glue, and paper to design different types of clouds (http://faculty.ssu.edu/sect7.htm). *June 29, 1999* (Wiesner, 1992) is recommended reading for classes learning about vegetables. Other activities for the book consist of making a graph of favourite vegetables, listing adjectives to describe them, and making vegetable soup; students are also asked to locate the different US states and cities mentioned in the story (Reading Rainbow Teachers Activities Episode #100 *June 29, 1999* gpn.unl.edu/guides/rr/100.pdf-). One can also find a website that suggests reading *Hurricane* (Wiesner, 1990) when learning about weather patterns (http://www.eduplace.com/tview/tviews/h/hurricane.html).

The second type of activity works beyond the particular text. One website suggests that classes write the words for *Tuesday* (http://faculty.ssu.edu/%7Eelbond/tuesday.htm#hor6); another asks students to write a continuation for either *Tuesday* or *Sector 7* (http://faculty.ssu.edu/(elbond/tues.htm). The Children's Art Activities website invites the class to read *Hurricane*, then examine the wallpaper in the main characters' room – which is the source of the protagonists' imaginary adventures – and later design their own wallpaper, keeping in mind adventures they would like to have (http://www.nccil.org/forchildren/txt_aa_dw.html). Students are also told to look for Wiesner's self-portrait in the same book, then to draw their own self-portraits. The class is also asked to imagine how the *June 29, 1999* space creatures' planet might look. A website for *The Three Pigs* (Wiesner, 2001) has students designing structures that would withstand extreme conditions (http://eduscapes.com/caldecott/02a.htm). Another recommends that students write a story about other folktale or fairytale characters that could be rescued by the three pigs (http://www.vickiblackwell.com/lit/threepigs/html).

These activities may lead to valid learning experiences for students. However, they fail to take into account the superb qualities of Wiesner's art itself. There is a shortage of activities that examine the elements of his picture books to determine how he creates stories with universal appeal. Despite Wiesner's countless awards as an author/illustrator, few resources investigate how he utilizes and designs each book's images and text to tell a story from a unique viewpoint and to engage the reader in the picture book experience.

Some websites do have activities that look at aspects of Wiesner's images. The Trumpet Club website for Grades 1–3 states that the pages in *Sector 7* (Wiesner, 1999) have a lot of visual information, yet only goes as far as to ask students to look at the book page by page and list what they notice (http://www.trumpetclub.com/primary/activities/sector7.htm). The Children's Art Activities site goes further, it explores the use of 'bird's eye view' as the viewpoint in *Tuesday* (http://www.nccil.org/forchildren/text_aa_dw.html). The Reading Rainbow site also asks the class to discuss Wiesner's use of different perspectives in his illustrations for *June 29, 1999* (Wiesner, 1992), such as close-up and long shots, bird's eye view, and ground level looking up (Reading Rainbow Teachers Activities Episode #100 *June 29, 1999*, gpn.unl.edu/guides/rr/100.pdf-). One website, a picture book illustrator study for Year 6 classes, comes closest to a possible systematic analysis of Wiesner's (and other authors') visual images. The unit has as one of its aims: 'To assist students to develop an awareness of the role of an illustrator and also of the media and illustrative techniques used by illustrators to render their messages in visual texts' (http://www.teachers.ash.org/au/bookzone/Docs/VisLit_tch.pdf-). The specific activities involve students in observing how Wiesner uses colour, shape and image size to convey a mood, as well as how he uses frames to create a film-like episode in *Tuesday* (Wiesner, 1991).

These four lessons available on the internet could be a good starting point to study the meaning in a picture book's images, thereby enriching class discussions about Wiesner's illustrative art. However, they could also remain perfunctory or peripheral activities if teachers and students do not have the means to discuss the meaning-making resources of images with some depth of understanding.

In their article 'Discussing text and illustration with others', Nancy J. Johnson and Cyndi Giorgis talk about how:

> readers . . . benefit from the support that discussion provides. This means that teachers and librarians can introduce literature with layers of meaning. Some books rely on language or text structures that read like a puzzle. Others present illustrations that hold the potential interpretation or texts that introduce situations that are not readily understood . . . reading and discussing such books with others can be illuminating and exciting.
>
> (2000: 109)

David Wiesner's picture books are a stimulating and rich source of imagery and unique points of view, and being able to discuss how his images create meaning for a viewer could be just as exciting and could help students develop a greater appreciation of the author/illustrator's craft. What is vital is that teachers and students have access to a language that can be used to discuss the semiotics of visual images:

> Teachers and students need . . . a language for talking about language, images, texts, and meaning-making interactions . . . to develop an educationally accessible functional grammar . . . a metalanguage that describes meaning in various realms. These include the textual and the visual, as well as the multimodal relations between the different meaning-making processes that are now so critical in media texts and the texts of electronic multimedia.
>
> (New London Group, 1996: 27)

We have provided an introduction to this kind of metalanguage in Chapter 1 and show its application later in this chapter in discussing the illustrated novel, *Dreamwalker* by Isobelle Carmody and Steven Woolman (2001). Further work using this metalanguage is dealt with in subsequent chapters.

Opportunities for readers' response

Many author websites encourage readers to communicate with the author by email. In most cases this does not mean direct email contact, but emails are frequently responded to by the author's posting of general responses to common email topics. This is the case with the Morris Gleitzman site referred to earlier. Some sites solicit children's reviews of books, which can be typed on screen on the website and submitted electronically, as is the case on the Roald Dahl site (http://www.roalddahl.com/index3.htm). Specialist children's literature websites (http://www.acs.ucalgary.ca/~dkbrown/) include links to online discussion groups for children where they can submit reviews of books and read reviews of others. Some publishers' websites encourage submission of responses to aspects of particular books, such as the current 'Harry Potter' discussion issue on the Scholastic site (http://www.scholastic.com/harrypotter/home.asp – retrieved 4 April 2004):

> In *Harry Potter and the Order of the Phoenix* Harry had dreams about walking down a hallway to a door. Eventually when he stumbled across the real hallway in the Department of Mysteries, he realized this dream was a premonition. Have you ever had a dream that turned out to be a premonition? Describe the dream and whether it helped you.

We will consider children's participation in on-line discussion groups more in Chapter 3.

Participation in book-related activities such as game-playing and purchase of book merchandising

Downloading of screensavers, book plates and copies of artefacts from stories are very much part of the web-world of children's literature. Competitions are conducted on-line, such as Scholastic's 'Wizard Challenge' (http://www.scholastic.com/kids/games.htm), where participants can test their 'Harry Potter' knowledge. Electronic games related to fictive narratives are now not only becoming a common part of the post narrative experience, but are also becoming part of a suite of experiences comprising the initial introduction of new narratives. We referred earlier to the popular *Wicked* stories of Paul Jennings and Morris Gleitzman. On Paul Jennings' website (http://www.paul jennings.com.au/ – retrieved 4 April, 2004), he now asks visitors 'Why don't you check out our "Wicked" animations? Here you can meet Rory, Dawn and the Appleman or have a go at squashing the SLOBBERERS.'

Jon Scieszka and Lane Smith are probably best known for their metafictive work, *The Stinky Cheese Man and Other Fairly Stupid Tales* (Scieszka and Smith, 1992). Their website (http://www.baloneyhenryp.com/ – retrieved 4 April

2004) currently promotes their new book, *Henry P. Baloney* and included on the site is an electronic game entitled 'Henry's Piskas Game'.

The prominent role of electronic games in concert with children's literature as a marketing strategy can be clearly seen in the Penguin site for young readers   (http://www.penguinputnam.com/static/packages/us/yreaders-new/featuredbooksites-start.html – retrieved 4 April 2004):

> Welcome to the Penguin Group for Young Readers Featured Book Sites portal. Here, you'll find all of your favorite Penguin Putnam characters, from Peter and Fudge to Winnie-the-Pooh. There are activities, interviews, reading tips, screensavers, and on-line games! What are you waiting for?

Learning activities with Isobelle Carmody's *Dreamwalker*: on-line/off-line

In this section we will first of all consider a range of on-line resources that could be used to support classroom work with the gripping novel *Dreamwalker* by Isobelle Carmody, richly illustrated by Steve Woolman (2001). A lot of fascinating learning experiences can be generated using these resources but there remains a paucity of material which addresses the actual narrative art entailed in the textual construction of the story through language and image. We will therefore also indicate the kind of complementary off-line learning activities that can develop learners' engagement with an appreciation of the literary 'constructedness' of the novel.

Surveying on-line resources

The fascinating story and striking images of *Dreamwalker* will appeal to readers from about 10 years of age to adulthood. The narrator, Ken, is a young adolescent who has been an insomniac since childhood. His driving interest is drawing and his ambition is to become an artistic composer of comic books. His long waking hours in the night are largely spent drawing stories and on one such occasion he creates the sorceress, whose vampire-like minions, which emanate from her dreams, feed on unwitting sleepers. One day Ken wakes from a dream and finds himself in the world he has created, where one of his characters, the beautiful Alyssa, claims to have imagined him in a dream. As the intricate plot unfolds, we are drawn into an incredible situation where it becomes impossible, even for Ken, to tell who is the creator, who has been dreamed and who is the dreamer.

The main potential of the www resources for enhancing classroom activities with *Dreamwalker* is the facilitation of work with children on intertextuality – exploring related texts dealing with similar themes. Biographical notes about the author and information on the context of composition of the story are very limited on the websites of publishers (http://www.penguin.com.au/puffin/default.htm) and booksellers (http://www.fantasticfiction.co.uk/authors/Isobelle_Carmody.htm) retrieved in April 2004. Promotion of the book and engagement of readers on these sites rely only on cover illustrations and brief reviews/synopses. Learning activities are included on one of the publisher's sites (http://www.lothian.com.au). These include a summary of the plot and a list of suggested tasks for students, which include some 'response' to aspects of the novel, but appear, for the most part, like a series of 'comprehension questions' that presuppose students' capacity to compose answers rather than scaffolding them to appreciate how the language and images of the text create its interpretive possibilities.

1) Ken is the main character. Do a pen portrait of him outlining the type of person he is. Touch on his background, what interests him, his skills and his ambitions and occupations.
2) Where does Ken get his ideas?
3) What effect does this story have on Ken? What effect do the characters, particularly the two Alyssas, have on him?
   . . . .
6) Who is the 'Deformed One' referred to in Chapter 3? Why is this epithet used?
7) Describe the sorceress and her role in the story.
8) Who is the bard? What part does the bard play?
               (Extract from Teachers' Notes, http://www.lothian.com.au
                                        – retrieved 4 April 2004)

Searching beyond publishers' sites revealed the range of resources that could be used for intertextual work related to *Dreamwalker*. The sites included another children's novel and a comic book – both with the same title and a related theme, a free e-book on-line, a gallery of a science fiction and fantasy art including a work entitled 'Dreamwalker', as well as on-line role-playing games and clubs with the same title and themes (see Chapter 4 for other examples of on-line role playing game narratives).

The summary information for the *Dreamwalker* comic series indicates its potential for intertextual study with Carmody and Woolman's *Dreamwalker*:

Karen Brinson is a Dreamwalker, capable of projecting herself into the dreams of others. It is an ability she is learning to control with the help of Mrs Tobias, her eccentric neighbour and closet psychic. But dreamscapes can be fragile, delicate places. Karen must be careful not to trespass and do serious and irreparable harm to the psyche of the person whose dreamworld she has entered. Five issues of this series were previously published by Dreamwalker Press. The Tapestry series begins all-new stories and is the perfect jumping on point for new readers.

(http://www.calibercomics.com/Checkout4Pro/dreamweaver.htm – retrieved 15 May 2003)

The free on-line e-book, *The Dreamwalker's Daughter*, also has clear intertextual connections with the Carmody and Woolman story (and with the Harry Potter stories):

Sarah made it through her first year at Dragon's Wood with a lot of help from her friends. All she wants is a year without nightmares and what she finds out about herself makes her long for the days of nightmares and dreamless sleep potions.

(http://www.thedarkarts.org/authors/tproctor/DD01.html – retrieved 4 April 2004)

The science fiction and fantasy artist, Cally G. Steussy has created a work called 'Dreamwalker', and on her website includes a short narrative about her picture:

Nesaka was just a poor girl, orphaned by bandits and raised by an innkeeper who only kept her because it meant an unpaid pair of hands. Then her magic began to bloom. She has the ability to walk in dreams, as well as normal magic – but at times, HER dreams decide to walk the waking world, and cannot be defeated until she awakens. Nesaka despaired of ever learning to control her powers, and honestly considered giving up, until she met her soulmate – another dreamwalker. The two met often in dreams, until one day a powerful dream grabbed both of them and became reality (that's where Nesaka found her staff, btw). They escaped the dream, and were rescued by a pair of sorcerers from a school of magic. Now they're learning how to use their magic, and how to keep their pasts from using them.

(http://elfwood.lysator.liu.se/loth/s/t/steussy/nesaka1clrsz.jpg.html – retrieved 4 April 2004)

Much of this material the students can engage with directly on-line. This is not possible with the comic books, although some teachers may explore purchasing these. Using only the materials directly available on the www, students can consider which aspects of the Dreamwalker stories are common in terms of plot, theme and character. Clearly there are some similarities between the comic book heroine, Karen Brinson, and the character Nesaka, behind the picture created by Cally Steussy. Themes of the Dreamwalkers using their powers to defeat forces of evil permeate some of the on-line materials as well as the Carmody and Woolman story. The images on the web can also be used to complement exploration of the Steve Woolman images. The second novel entitled *Dreamwalker* by Mary Summer Rain (1993) was located on a bookseller's site (http://www.hamptonroadspub.com/bookstore/product_info.php?products_id=61). The cover of this book, shown on the website, has some visual features that are quite similar to those used by Steve Woolman in his depiction of the sorceress on the cover of Carmody's *Dreamwalker*, which can be seen on the publishers site (http://www.lothian.com.au). The Cally Steussy image is very different from both of these, and comparison can be used to initiate an exploration of the ways in which the language and images in the Carmody and Woolman book are selected to reflect the uncertainty (on the part of the narrator, Ken, and the readers!) as to what is occurring in the dream world and what is occurring in the 'real' world.

We mentioned earlier how electronic games were fast becoming part of the context of composition of children's literature as well as part of the context of extended merchandising. While this is not directly the case with *Dreamwalker*, games and role-playing on-line are certainly part of the wider intertextual context of the stories. One on-line role-playing game is entitled 'Dreamwalker: Roleplaying in the land of dreams'. The brief scenario for the game indicates the intertextual connections to much of the material we have discussed:

> Humanity is under attack. The enemy is an alien species that assails us in our most vulnerable state – while we sleep. The Taenia Spiritus are a race of soulless, hive-minded creatures that invade our dreams in order to foster and feed off the negative vibes and emotions caused by their presence.
>
> You are a Dreamwalker. Whether by drugs, prayer, meditation or natural ability, you are able to leave your own dreams and travel into the Dreamworlds of others. Once there you can manipulate the dream's spiritual energy, or mana, to produce wondrous effects.
>
> You have been recruited by Project Dreamwalker – a government-backed organization that unites others like you in order to rid the spirit world of the Taeniid plague. The task is difficult. Not only do you face the Taenia but you must also satisfy the whims and desires of the Dreamer in whose mind they are ensconced. Can you do this and still maintain a grasp on your own sanity?
>
> Good luck, Dreamwalker. You may be our last hope.
> (http://dreamwalkerrpg.home.att.net/ – retrieved 4 April 2004)

Again, even if students do not participate in the game, the directly available on-line materials, including synopses and the images on the introductory website are the kinds of resources that can provoke new perspectives on reading the novel itself.

Although more tenuously linked to the notions underlying the Carmody and Woolman *Dreamwalker*, students may be interested to visit the 'Dreamwalker Holt' – an on-line role-playing/collaborative story composition site:

> The Dreamwalkers are a pure-blooded, reindeer-riding elf tribe living on the tundra and in the mountains of northern Junsland, long before the continent was named. We are called Dreamwalkers because we 'Journey' in the 'spirit world' with the help of the Crystals. (A little like human Shamanism!)
>
> Dreamwalkers' Holt is a (mostly!) Swedish on-line Holt.
>
> (http://www.randomdice.com/dreamwalkersholt/menu.asp
> – retrieved 4 April 2004)

The site publishes guidelines for story contributions, which are common to many such sites but indicate the key character role of Dreamwalkers very early in the list:

> # Each member may have one 'personal' character who is currently alive. Other characters you create will have to be adoptables or characters common to the Holt, except for a child/children too young to leave the parent(s). (Up to around ten or twelve years of age.) However, there's lots of history to play with!
>
> # No wanderers allowed (for now – we may have some ideas for later on!). Your character has to be a Dreamwalker, a Two Rivers' Wolfrider or a 'halfbreed'. (Or possibly a Troll!) (This also means that we'll never run into Cutter's tribe, for example!)

There are several sites celebrating Carmody's work and including images of her (for example, http://www.skynet.net.au – 4 April 2004) and some including discussion boards where readers can post comments and questions about her books (http://www.allreaders.com). The latter are opportunities for learners to publish perspectives on *Dreamwalker* not dealt with on other sites. One such perspective is an appreciation of the verbal and visual 'constructedness' of the narrative art, which teachers can assist children to develop using the functional resources of visual and verbal grammar outlined in Chapter 1.

Exploring the use of image and language in *Dreamwalker* off-line

In this section we will briefly focus on developing children's understanding of the interactive or interpersonal meanings constructed by images and text and how these influence our interpretive responses to the text. First, we explore the interactive meanings of three images at the beginning of the story, and then we will explore the role of interpersonal meanings in the language of two segments later in the novel – one when Ken and Alyssa in the dream world are trying to work out what the sorceress is trying to do, and one when Ken and Alyssa in the real world are beginning to negotiate closer sharing with each other.

The images we will consider are of two of the main characters – the sorceress depicted on the cover of the book (Figure 2.1) and then the images of the sorceress and the narrator, Ken, on the first double-page spread of Chapter 1 (Figure 2.2). Our approach would be to model the application of the grammar of interactive meanings in images using the front cover image of the sorceress and then scaffold the children's application of these grammatical concepts to interpreting the images on the first double-page spread of Chapter 1.

We might begin by noting that this cover picture of the sorceress is a narrative image and that the main processes are screaming, violent tossing of the head and flailing of the arms. The tossing and flailing are indicated by the vectors or action lines shown in grey as the rapidly changing positions of the head and arms. Then in terms of interactive meanings we might ask the children where they would be positioned if they were with the sorceress and they actually took this image as a photograph. This enables them to understand the vertical position – they are positioned below the sorceress as if she has power over them. They are also positioned at an oblique angle to her frontal plane, so there is no feeling of inclusion with her, they are not part of her world. In addition, she is not looking directly at them, so there is no contact or demand for interaction. They are observing her rather than interacting with her.

Then we might ask the children to consider these questions about inter-active/interpersonal meanings in relation to the first double-page spread. The children will notice that they are positioned quite differently in relation to these images than they were positioned in relation to the cover image. By thinking about this difference in terms of the vertical and horizontal angles of the images and whether the images are offers or demands, the children will be able to articulate how the meaning-making resources of the images are deployed to construct them as viewers in this different position. There are, of course, many other features of the images at work that also contribute to this positioning of the viewer, but space will not permit us to pursue these here.

We can examine the interpersonal resources of the language in a somewhat similar manner. Again we would model the examination of the interpersonal grammar and then provide an opportunity for the children to apply this know-ledge to another segment of the story. In the short passage below from page 31 of the novel, Ken and Alyssa in the dream world are reasoning about the intention of the sorceress.

Figure 2.1 *Dreamwalker* Cover

Figure 2.2 The sorceress and Ken

01 Alyssa gave a queer, rumbling sound that startled Ken until he
understood that she was growling.
02 'This is evil news indeed.
03 She was trying to establish a link to your world.
04 [Perhaps] you are right in thinking it was partly her magic that
drew you here.
05 That [could] also explain
06 why the guards were searching tonight.
07 They were looking for you.'
08 Ken's skin broke into a chilly sweat of fear.
09 'It becomes more important than ever to try to get you away
from here,'
10 Alyssa said.
11 'If she has you,
12 she [will] use you
13 to establish a path to your world.'

In Alyssa's initially uncertain speculation we notice the use of the low modal
adverb 'Perhaps' and the low modal verb 'could'. Then in clause 7 she is more
confident about her deduction and the modals and modal adverbs disappear.
Then in her confident knowledge in clauses 11–13 the high modal 'will'
appears. Through this kind of discussion the children can learn how speculation and uncertainty are realized grammatically and the grammatical means
by which this is changed to being sure and confident. Following this kind of
discussion the children might be asked to consider quite a different context
where modal adverbs and verbs feature prominently, such as the following
segment from page 44 when Alyssa in the real world and Ken are beginning to
negotiate a closer sharing with each other:

01 'Imagine
02 if I wanted to write a poem about this whole thing that happened
to you.'
03 'It [would] be an epic poem.'
04 'It [could] be,
05 but I [would] want to try to tell everything in a few perfect
words.'
06 Ken looked at her slyly.
07 'I'd [really] like it
08 if you showed me one of your poems.'
09 She gave him a sharp look.
10 'Well [maybe.']
11 She bit her lip.
12 'I've been wanting to ask you something.'

It may help some children to have the modal verbs and adverbs highlighted and to focus on the effects of these choices. Alyssa's use of 'could' in clause 4 accepts Ken's suggestion even though in the next clause she indicates her preference for another form of communicating Ken's experience. Children might also consider the role of the intensifier 'really' by Ken and what the effect would be if this were simply omitted, or if some alternative was used, such as 'kind of'. Similarly, they could consider the effect of 'maybe' in clause 10, by imagining other possible endings of that clause and how these would impact on interpreting the relation between the two characters.

In working with *Dreamwalker* the www resources provide primarily opportunities for 'going beyond the text' whereas learning experiences involving students 'getting into the text' needed to be generated off-line. At present, our view is that this is likely to be the case for most children's books, but as teachers and children look more at the role of language and images in the narrative art of children's literature, perhaps there will be more www-based resources oriented to 'getting into the text'.

Conclusion

In this chapter the emphasis has been on children's literary texts available in electronic format and on-line resources supporting teaching and learning about children's literature. We have briefly noted opportunities for children to produce on-line responses to literary texts. In the next two chapters we focus on children's on-line discussion of literature and their collaborative on-line production of multimodal narratives.

3 Booktalk 'on-line'
Learning about literature through 'book raps'

Introduction

In this chapter we introduce the widely successful concept of book raps – a programme involving children talking about books with others using electronic media of email and web-based discussion forums. The chapter starts by outlining reasons why teachers have found the use of book raps such a valuable addition to their existing classroom practices involving talking about books. The response from teachers has been extremely positive, as they have observed first hand the potential of book raps. As a direct result of their interactive design, book raps have stimulated children's enthusiasm and enjoyment of books, bringing about more complex modes of communication and therefore more complex appreciation of texts. To demonstrate this potential, a programme for working on-line with literary texts is described and instructions are given about how to take part in a book rap for the first time. Finally, examples of different kinds of involvement with raps are outlined and a number of international websites hosting book raps are indicated.

Why discussions on the net?

The essence of a book rap is to take the best of classroom work with literary texts and make it available to more students. The basic model could be run within a school via an intranet. The only requirements are that someone plan a unit of work based on a literary text that includes questions to stimulate rich discussion, and that this person also provides input for teachers to use to frame up their lessons, and is ready to sum up and answer questions from book rap participants.

In the ideal book rap model children still interact with texts to examine the construction of story through print and image, but as well as speaking to children in their own classroom, they interact with others who come from different geographical locations. The means of interaction is via the internet on email lists. This style of interaction has a number of benefits: it creates new communities of learners, aligns with favoured contemporary modes of communication among young people, encourages reflective participation, facilitates involvement of those not at ease with face-to-face communication and has the bonus of providing a written record of interactions for later evaluation.

Alongside the increasing use of ICT, the reading of books remains a very popular and culturally highly valued activity. The enduring attraction of reading stories to children and young people is clearly nurtured through the work of their teachers sharing books with them. Book raps do not replace this important face-to-face sharing of reading and learning through literature. They build on it by deepening the students' potential responses to text through engagement in meaningful conversations with others. This is partly achieved by the vastly increased audience for students' shared responses on-line and the potential broader range of interactants including older and younger students as well as teachers in other schools – often in other countries. Book raps offer a means of creating an on-line community that 'meets' regularly to discuss literary texts in such a way that critique, comparison and shared understanding are made possible through reciprocal patterns of interaction. Through an on-line framework students from different geographical locations who have read the same book are guided through a staged sequence of discussion activities by a rap coordinator.

However, the benefits of book raps are not just an increased number of readers talking about the same book. Raps have also increased the depth of readers' literary understanding through a combination of on-line, guided learning and in-class teacher support. The story below told by a classroom teacher illustrates one encounter with book raps where a combination of on-line conversation, scaffolded tasks and guided learning led to the creation of a positive literacy experience for one unmotivated reader:

Simon's story

As part of a book rap in 2001, eleven- and twelve-year-old children were asked to write reviews on the Children's Book Council short-listed picture books for the year and post them to the email list. In the class where I was teaching, I modelled review writing, we worked on joint construction of reviews and then I gave each child a book to which they were meant to respond. One boy, a resistant reader and writer, wrote a very short and disparaging review of Tohby Riddle's book *The Singing Hat* based on his own personal feelings. He did not want to take part in the task as he found it annoying to read a picture book and engage with the text through writing. He posted his negative opinion and thought he had finished with the task. What he did not consider was that his posting would be read by other children of his own age, some of whom might have different opinions to him. The next library lesson when the children read the incoming emails there was one addressed directly to Simon. The writer, a peer of his own age, disagreed with him and gave some sound reasons why they thought the book was worthy of being on the short list. It caused an unexpected reaction. This was not a teacher who was marking his work for assessment purposes; this was another kid who was taking him on. I have never seen Simon so motivated to read closely and write. For the first time in his troubled literacy experiences, he reread a book and carefully argued his case, still negative but this time with a more complex rationale. Because of the complex interaction set up in the book rap, he was brought face to face with an unknown peer who wanted to have a conversation with him about a book. It was a moment of real engagement that was stunning to see.

If we consider Simon's story, we can see that there are two key elements that led to its positive outcome. The success of individual book raps depends as much on the programme of discussion that is shaped by the coordinator of the book rap as on the nature of the interaction that takes place in the classroom and on-line between rappers. Simon's interaction with a peer occurred because a student wrote back directly to him, yet this is not the usual pattern of connection in book raps where rappers mostly write back to the coordinator. His teacher had also carefully scaffolded his learning following the rap point set up by the coordinator so that he was prepared for the task which required him to consider the construction of the text he read. But what was new to his engagement with text was the on-line interaction.

Book raps have the potential to increase students' motivation to engage with literature and to increase the sophistication of their engagement, as demonstrated through the nature of their on-line shared, interactive responses. Fortunately, book raps are also one area where the application of ICT to classroom learning can be achieved without requiring teachers to have high levels of technological expertise. If as Turnbull reports (as quoted in Lankshear and Knobel, 2003: 70), teachers are hampered by lack of understanding of, and confidence in technology, then book raps will demonstrate how they need only learn some very simple technological skills to work on-line in the familiar teaching area of children's literature. The aim in introducing book raps here is to show one use of ICT in the classroom that provides 'transformational learning experiences for students' (Andrews, 2003) and to encourage teachers to try it out.

Background and essential features of book raps

In simple terms, a book rap is a conversation about reading a book that takes place on-line among school children over a number of weeks. Its main aim is to develop 'a love of literature by sharing books with children and having them share with each other' (Stubbs, 1999: 59). Although the term 'rap' has become most commonly associated with poetry or other modes of rhyming and often rhythmic spoken texts, in this case the term 'rap' is taken to mean talk. The adoption of the term 'rap' by the original designers signals the motivation of the rap organizers to break down traditional formats of classroom work with literary texts to create the possibility of more open communication among a broader range of readers.

Begun in 1996 as an on-line curriculum project with Oz-projects, book raps have emerged as a key example of purposeful e-literacy practice in Australia (Simpson, 2004; Stubbs, 1999). The raps provide an opportunity for students to develop a wide range of language skills as they read books, defend their personal point of view, justify choices and review texts. They have been used successfully in Australia with children and young people ranging from the first to the final years of schooling to construct interactive critical literacy events with students beyond their own classroom and across a diverse range of communities. Raps conducted in recent years are listed in Table 3.1.

The two rap sites discussed in this chapter were created in Australia by the New South Wales Department of Education (NSW DET) and the Queensland University of Technology (QUT). The address for the QUT book raps from 2000–2005 is http://rite.ed.qut.edu.au/old_oz-teachernet/projects/book-rap/.

Table 3.1 Examples of titles on rap lists from the Queensland University of Technology and the Department of Education and Training NSW run in 2001–2003

Year	Run in Queensland	Run in NSW
2001	Teddy book rap	*Big Mob Dreaming – The Bunyip*
2001	*Bob the Builder and the Elves*	*The Binna Binna Man*
2001	*Fantastic Mr Fox*	Book Week – Picture books
2002	*Someone Like Me*	Henry Lawson
2002	*A Pet for Mrs Arbuckle*	Book Week – Early childhood
2002	*Harry Potter and the Philosopher's Stone*	*Harry Potter and the Chamber of Secrets*
2003	*Njunjul the Sun*	*Only the Heart*
2003	*Hating Alison Ashley*	*Wilfred Gordon McDonald Partridge*

The NSW DET book raps site is http://www.schools.nsw.edu.au/schoollibraries/teaching/raps/.

It is the commitment of physical space on a server, the human support of a webmaster and participant access to the internet that allow the raps to take place. The server hosts the website that students make contact with; the webmaster keeps and maintains the files that format the structure of the rap as a series of web pages and email lists; and the internet makes it possible to connect individual computers together so that students can interact. A teacher joining a rap needs access to a computer with an internet connection. This could be in the classroom, in the library or at home. To take part in a rap, the teacher or responsible child will need to be able to log on to a website, enter a password, access and post emails.

Each rap focuses on a particular story and has its own coordinator. The coordinator is a volunteer who has offered to create and run a rap. This means they will choose the text for the rap, design the rap and be responsible for answering the emails that are sent in. At the developmental stage, the rap coordinator makes decisions about: the age level that the rap will be suggested for; the kinds of questions and activities that they will create; the possibility of using live links to other sites for resources; the benefits of connections to authors, illustrators and other experts; and when the rap will be run. The book choice may be based on curriculum knowledge, favourite author, recently published book, or some other rationale. An introductory message is written inviting students to join the rap. It gives details about the coordinator so that students know to whom they are writing.

A series of rap points is also written by the rap coordinator. These are questions that will guide the students through their interaction with the text. After the coordinator has designed the questions for the rap, they are then sent to a webmaster. The webmaster is the person in control of the rap projects at the host site. It is the webmaster's responsibility to assess the suggested outlines and call for amendments according to site policy. Although the rap coordinator has authority to approve the shaping of the rap, the webmaster has the final authority to approve the content and format of the rap. Feedback from the webmaster to the rap coordinator may include requests to align the rap points with particular curriculum requirements, to edit language to accord with certain syllabus expectations or to broaden the interactive scope of the rap by adding in more links. When the changes have been made, the webmaster then transfers the information into a formalized structure for each particular website and posts it live to the net. Each rap is advertised on-line in summary form with details such as: when the rap is to start, when the rap points are to be posted, what the rap points are to be, the publishing details of the book, the age suitability of the rap participants, the coordinator's name and resource links to other sites or to support materials for teaching. A calendar of upcoming raps allows teachers to select the rap that they wish to join with time for planning the incorporation of the rap into their usual programming for work with literature in the classroom.

There is a language that is particular to the organization of the rap. It creates a culture and history for those involved and is a kind of code that is internal to the rap to signal the different activities to complete and to signify that those who take part are a special group. The specialist terms include: rap point, rappers, rap map, rap wrap up. It is clear that the words are used to construct a self-referential vocabulary that will be recognized only by those who have taken part in a rap. The use of the language creates a means of identifying and being identified with the system. For example, a rap sheet is the on-line version of a black line master, prepared before the rap starts as support material for teachers to use. A rap map is one of the features encouraged for use in the book raps where participating rappers create a map to track where the emails that they receive are coming from. It is a tangible reminder that their communication is traveling far and wide (or just to the next suburb in some cases).

An essential part of the book raps are the email lists that are set up for participants to communicate with the moderator and with each other. There are two main lists, one for the students to post their responses to the rap points and the other for teachers to discuss their work on the rap with each other. The teacher list has closed access for teachers only, while the student list is open to students, teachers, the rap coordinator and other participants and observers. The student email list receives the communication from the rap coordinator. This takes the form of the initial introduction, the rap points, rap point feedback and finally the rap wrap up. The student email list also receives the responses from participants wishing to respond to the rap points or others' messages. Responses may be sent as messages from whole classes, small groups or individuals. The choice depends on how the teachers are running the rap in their classroom – whether it is for the whole class or as an extension reading activity or special option for those who wish to join.

When students respond to the rap points, all their emails are posted on this email list. The potential is there for all list members to receive all the emails sent to this list. This can amount to a very large number of emails to read, so management of incoming and outgoing messages is an issue for teachers. What computer is used to send and receive emails? Who collects the emails? Who reads the emails? Who sends the emails? These are all issues that need resolving within each teacher's personal plan for the rap. In raps with large numbers of participants, instead of reading all emails, some schools only read the responses from a chosen number of schools. The decision also needs to be taken whether to print out all emails or read them on screen. This limits the number of people who can read the emails easily, so again it is a management issue.

Teachers may nominate to join their own dedicated list as an addition to the student list. The email list for the teachers is used to provide further support for teachers. Its main purpose is to provide a forum for teachers that may be used to discuss educational issues. The webmaster will monitor this list to provide technological advice for those who report that they are having problems. It is commonly used to discuss teaching strategies and for sharing of ideas and activities. The teachers' email list receives communication from the rap coordinator but not the same messages sent to the children. The coordinator's messages to the teachers are to further explain the rap points or point out any special preparation there might be for participation. The quantity of postings on the teachers' list is much less than that on the students' list.

As well as links to current raps, the websites for the raps may also carry links to records of past book raps. If still live, these archives are made available for general viewing. They show the rap points and the responses to display how the discussion ran and to make it possible for those who did not take part to make use of questions or other resources some time after the event.

It is easy to plan a programme of work around a book rap, as there is a set procedure that occurs for each rap. This is summarized in Table 3.2.

Table 3.2 An overview of steps to participate in a book rap: timeframe 4–6 weeks

Teacher	Coordinator	Students
Chooses rap from selection and joins list. Introduces book to students	Designs rap and submits it to webmaster	Read book
Prepares introduction with students	Sends rap introduction	Respond to coordinator by writing introduction including: name of school, location and message of welcome from students to other schools
Note location of other rap schools Works with students on rap point 1	Sums up introduction messages and posts rap point 1	Use rap map to mark where schools are. (not obligatory) Respond to introductions from other schools. (not obligatory) Respond to rap point 1 in discussion and then email
Works with students on rap point 2	Summarizes responses and posts rap point 2	Respond to rap point 2 in discussion and then email
Works with students on rap point 3	Summarizes responses and posts rap point 3	Respond to rap point 3 in discussion and then email
Finishes off with rap wrap up comment to class	Summarizes responses and posts rap wrap up	Complete rap wrap up work

The entire series of rap points and in some cases suggested teaching activities is presented on-line weeks before the commencement of the rap. This allows for forward planning for the teacher to develop a set of lessons that are framed around the rap points. It is possible for one teacher to run a rap in her/his own room or for a librarian to run all of the same age group through the same rap using similar lesson plans. It would be equally possible for a group of teachers teaching on the same age group to take it in turns to programme for raps since the core of the preparation work is already done. Teachers may choose the book they wish to base their unit of work on by accessing the rap calendar, which lists what will be available for each term of the school year. For example, the list for the New South Wales Department of Education and Training raps in 2001 showed the choice of a range of books for different ages over the year: Big Mob Dreaming – The Bunyip (*Big Mob Dreaming – The Bunyip*, 1997) for children aged 6–7 years, *Mrs Millie's Painting* (Ottley, 1997) for children aged 8–9 years, the Children's Book Council short-listed picture books for children aged 10–12 years, *Binna Binna Man* (McDonald, 1999) for students aged 14–15 years, and *Othello* (Bentley, 1982) for students aged 16–17 years.

Enhancing 'talk about text' through book raps

Soldier on the Hill by Jackie French (1997) was the subject of a rap conducted in 2000. A sample from this rap is shown in Figure 3.1. It demonstrates how in the first rap point instructions were given to older primary school students that carefully positioned them to consider the verbal construction of the text. The moderator led the readers to appreciate French's use of sensory verbs and adjectives in order for them to engage more deeply with the experience of the main character.

Talking about literary texts has long been seen as a useful way to encourage students to read texts and read them more closely and critically. Two key approaches to talk about text in the classroom that have been successfully used by teachers are Chambers 'Tell me' questions (Chambers, 1985) and Daniels' literature circles (Daniels, 2002). These models of book talk are quite different. Although they both ask readers to talk, they employ talk for contrasting purposes.

Chambers' famous 'Tell me' questions focus attention on the way that children may be prompted to reflect on their responses to a text after reading it. For example, the question 'Who was telling the story?' asks the child to consider the construction of point of view in a narrative. Instead of just accepting their first impression of a character, the question 'Did we ever get to know what the characters were thinking about?' suggests the possibility of other reasons behind a turn in the plot. 'Does anyone know anything about the

Hi rappers,
I am so keen to have you start to think about the book that I am going to ask you to think about two things in one rap point. One is about the writing of the text and the other is about the background information. I am assuming that you haven't had time to read the whole book yet so the first rap point can be answered even if you have only read chapters 1–2.

Rap point one: (a)
Jackie French is a writer who writes so that you can hear/see/feel what it is like to be the character (if you don't believe me read Someone Like Me). My first challenge to you is to think about the words she uses to do that. For example, when we first meet Joey at the start of the book Jackie French describes the scene so that we know exactly what has happened without her saying so directly. Examine the text to see what you could draw/paint, record as sound effects or gather together to touch after reading the first chapter. Limit yourself only to what she describes and then see what incredible detail she has given you.

Once you have done that, write for yourself the beginning of a story which builds a similar amount of sensory detail for the reader. Why is it so important?

Figure 3.1   Rap point 1 for *Soldier on the Hill* rap

writer?' raises issues of cultural context concerning the historical perspective a writer might give to a particular topic. 'Have you read other books like this one?' asks children to make connections between texts via a range of comparative elements. The mix of open-ended questions that Chambers offers to teachers shifts the level of response from simple, factual recall to more complex empathy and deeper textual awareness. These questions may be used with any text and any grouping of children.

The example in Figure 3.2 demonstrates the kind of responses given in a rap where a directed but open-ended question was asked. The students need to have the prior knowledge necessary to deal with these kinds of questions. Some of the language is provided as scaffolding, and links to other sources of information are given, but the basic premise is that teacher will have already prepared their students to be able to bring into play a metalinguistic approach to written text and visual image, consistent with the orientation described in Chapter 1. The following responses indicate that the children were able to take the direction of the rap point into their classroom, spend time looking closely at the text and then write their own texts making use of the same techniques as Jackie French. The students show that they were able to develop deep textual awareness in this context.

> *I was sucking on a green sour tasting gooseberry when I tripped over a sharp twig and fell on to a sharp prickle on a gooseberry tree. Ouch the prickles were jabbing into the back of my legs. Blood was running down my legs. I was seeing rabbits jump slowly across my face I was fainting.*
>
> *One cold winder night, I could hear the soft touch of rain on the tin roof and the trickle of water running down the gutter. I could hear the owls hooting outside. The rain is gradually dying down and the sun is beginning to rise. I lay in my bed and look at the sunrise. My alarm went off and I gradually but slowly got out of bed. I slowly drifted down the creaky old staircase.*

Figure 3.2   Student responses to rap point one shown in Figure 3.1

By contrast, Daniels' literature circles (Daniels, 2002) are not organized by questions but by the roles that each reader in a small group is assigned during the reading of the book. The roles are related to tasks that are completed in response to the text. For example, the word wizard researches word use in the text, the artful artist depicts a part of the text in some kind of media. Literature circles were first designed to encourage independent reading and collaborative learning (Daniels, 2002) as a kind of interactive reading opportunity run in small groups in the classroom environment. At the start of a literature circle the readers nominate to join a particular group to discuss a book that they select. The group nomination of a text is viewed as a key factor in the success of these reading activities. The children read the text while carrying out their role and then after the reading is completed, each child has the responsibility to report back to the group. Talk in this situation is used to share what has been learnt but not to reinterpret the text.

The rap point 1(b) from the *Soldier on the Hill* rap shown in Figure 3.3 demonstrates a different focus from rap point 1(a). In point 1(b) readers were asked to share what they had learned from background reading, considering the cultural context and genesis of the story.

> *When Joey is rescued by the stranger, he is afraid of him because of his race and speaks of him in a way which we would not consider appropriate now. What is the historical background to the events on the story that makes it possible/likely that Joey would be feeling that way about someone who saves his life? Use books or the research website listed on the book rap intro page for information on Australia at the time of the story. Write a short summary of the reasons behind Joey's attitude.*

Figure 3.3   Rap point 1(b)

Just before the end of this rap, a teacher wrote to comment on the children's learning (Figure 3.4). She refers to the third rap point they have just finished and notes that it has created an extension activity for the students to explore after the rap finishes. She was excited by the literacy experiences that had been created for her students by someone other than her in a context that encouraged a lot of discussion and active reflection both in the classroom and on the email list.

We spent some time doing – Compare and contrast Joey's lifestyle with theirs. We will use this information for each child to do a brief 'time window' role play.

We are looking forward to the final rap point. There have been lots of great learning outcomes and the children have been motivated to think about a variety of subjects and consider their own thoughts and responses to some of the situations that Joey experiences.

Figure 3.4   Teacher reflection on the rap

Including book raps in classroom units of work

This section provides an example of how a particular book rap was integrated into a classroom programme of work. The Children's Book Council (CBC) short-list book rap from 2001 is used to demonstrate the programming that was needed to incorporate on-line work into a classroom programme for children aged 10–12 years. The lessons required familiarity with the books and the use of computers to type, compose word documents as well as access websites successfully and send emails. When the link was accessed for the CBC Book Week rap, a series of hypertexts presented the rap points and proforma in the form of work sheets that had been prepared to scaffold the rap across its seven weeks. It was then the teacher's responsibility to plan how the rap points would fit into the literacy programme that would run across the whole term of ten weeks. As the dates of the rap points were published before term started, the teacher knew there was time to work with the students to prepare them for the rap before they were expected to send any emails to the list. With this knowledge the teacher was able to organize a guest speaker in the previous term so that the students would have already been alerted to the topic.

The main aim of this book rap was to encourage critical analysis of techniques used by writers to create certain effects, to use language creatively, to position the reader in various ways and to construct different interpretations of experience. The programme of work including the book rap is outlined in a format typical of teachers' records of their planning of such units (see Box 3.1).

Box 3.1   Book Week programme

Focus area and rap points	Lesson structure
Previous experience to build field knowledge Guest speaker and book reading in library	A professional movie reviewer (a parent within the school) was invited to speak to all the children in the age group in the school as preparation for this literacy unit. He had recently published a review of the newly released movie *Spider Man* in a national newspaper. He spoke of the writing process from interview, to notes, to draft, to published form. He also talked about audience expectations, special effects, actors, marketing and plot construction in answer to questions raised by students. The students at this stage were not aware of the book rap focus but did know that they were expected to learn about reviews during the year as one of the set of required text types. The librarian has introduced the short-listed books to the students during the previous term. They have all heard the books read out loud and seen the images in a whole-class situation but have not looked closely at the texts themselves.
Lesson 1 Introduction to review texts as type of response. Reading and writing review texts	The teacher revises social purpose and organizational staging of response texts. This includes discussion of the grammatical features needed to construct structural elements of a review including the context in which the text is experienced, a description of the text, and a judgement about the text. The grammatical focus for this group was on the use of modality in expressing opinion, and noun groups with adjectival phrases for emphasis of detail.
Book rap is now live to the net School needs to register intention to take part.	Using an authentic example of a movie review for a recent movie that children would know, the teacher models the structure used. Students discuss purpose and audience given the context of publication (kids movie section of newspaper). They identify key structural features of the review and the verbal grammar used to create them.

Students are then given scaffolds designed according to their level of ability to construct a review of a simple chapter book that they have all recently read with the task of writing a review suitable to be placed in the library for younger children to read.

The lowest level scaffold is of the whole review cut up into different sentences. This group is also given another sheet that has section headings printed on it. The task is to regroup the sentences to achieve the correct structure as modelled. The middle group is given a scaffold with the section headings and the beginnings of sentences only. They are to complete the sentences with appropriate language to achieve the social purpose of the review. The top group is given section headings only and they must write the review using correct structure and grammar.

After independent writing time is up, groups made up of one or two from each level mix to compare their work for similarities and differences. The whole class then gathers for sharing and feedback. The reviews that are selected as appropriate will be published and placed with the book in the school library.

Lesson 2
Introduction to book rap topic.
Talking and listening about book awards.
Writing an introduction.

As a lead-up to the book week rap, the teacher introduces the topic of awards in relation to the books they have seen in the library. Students discuss the difference between the CBC awards that are awarded by adults for children's books and the Kids Own Australian Literature Awards that are awarded by children for children's books. They discuss how awards are given, who gives them and on what grounds. They discuss past CBC winners and whether they agreed with the judges' decision or not.

They talk about the role of a book judge and what they need to know to make their decisions. Students try to guess the judges' vote for this year given their knowledge of the books so far. When they realize that they need more information about the books to make a sound judgement, they discuss how they will be led to examine the books to see how the texts have been constructed visually and verbally.

Book rap week one rap requirements During the first week rappers send a short introductory message about their class or group and give some information about their school and its location. After reading other schools' introductions rappers locate schools on their Rap Map. If possible, introduce students to the six short-listed picture books. **Optional activities** Visit Children's Book Council site. Visit author and illustrator sites for background information. Commence rap journal writing.	Outline book rap to preview what tasks the children will have. That is to examine one text closely for its construction and then write a review judgement based on their scaffolded knowledge. Explain that their reviews will be sent to others who are taking part in a book rap following the same steps as them. In effect, it will be a chance for children to vote for the CBC books, so it is an authentic task. They will carry out this voting before the official results are published and then compare their comments with the judges. Remind them of visiting reviewer and his outline of his job and suggest they begin to take note of reviews in different contexts. Introduce book rap map to show how other schools will be tracked and then in small groups some compose a short introduction with basic details of class group to be posted on-line. One small group look on-line for other introductions to log on rap map. Another small group look on-line for background information from the CBC website. In whole class grouping compare introductions and compile 'best' bits. On-line groups report back on what introduction messages and/or information they have found. Rap map is displayed on wall for future reference and additions. A file is started on author information on the class computer and pages are book marked for others to read later.
Lesson 3 Looking closely at the construction of a text. Learning about visual grammar. Writing guided analysis of text and image. Writing guided personal response.	NB: Rap point one asks the students to look closely at the book *Fox* (Wild and Brooks, 2000) from the short-list and to use the proforma supplied on-line to carry out investigations focusing on verbal grammar and visual grammar. (The teacher may use these proforma or not but as they are designed to help all students within the rap community have the same experience of a text, it is a good idea to use them.)

To support the students' work before they start their guided group work, the teacher models a reading of *Fox*. Then, using key questions from rap points as guide, the teacher begins an examination of the text. The teacher first discusses the concept of cultural knowledge to help students interpret the images and text using clues from the vocabulary and images that match their everyday understandings. At this stage the students are only using what they already know to 'read' the text critically. They write a short individual response to the text to record this first reading referring to the clues they found.

Book rap week two
Rap Point 1

(a) In which country is this picture book set?

(b) What design features has the illustrator Ron Brooks utilized in the layout of *Fox*?

(c) The author Margaret Wild has dealt with several issues and themes throughout this book. What relevance do these issues have for you?

Then the students are introduced to some of the technical language available to describe their common sense readings. Terms such as: font, colour, layout are named as design features on the proforma to indicate use of specialist technical language. Their effects are discussed using other key terms. (Other terms have been introduced in previous lessons on visual grammar such as demand, offer, vectors, social distance.) Using these terms the students are asked to work in small groups and write a second response analyzing how the images contribute meaning to the text. They must look closely at the illustrations and verbal grammar to justify their decisions.

The third part of the lesson is an extension activity for those who may finish the two response texts quickly. Students are asked to write a short personal response text about how they believe the issues and themes of the book are relevant to them in the contexts of school and friendships. They are to discuss in small groups the real-life situations that they could describe as parallel with the action of the story. This kind of response moves the student away from role of text analyst and back towards text participant.

At the end of the lesson, the class forms as a whole again to compare responses given for parts b and c. These responses are then collated with responses from part a, and posted to the rap list.

Lesson 4 Reading books. Talking and listening about reviews. Writing guided review. **Book rap week three** **Rap Point 2** Which of the short-listed picture books is the class' or groups' favourite? Construct a written review of the text selected.	As a whole class, brainstorm the criteria used to assess each picture book for a review. Students complete proforma 1 for Rap Point 2. Teacher then names mixed ability groups to work on texts. Each group is given one of the short-listed books to reread. Students examine their nominated picture books and record comments on proforma. Using the scaffold from previous lessons on text construction, students then write a review of their book. At the end of the lesson the whole class gathers to hear the group reviews. Based on a discussion of the reviews given, the class votes to determine which title will be the class favourite and the book that they would award the first prize to. The group decision is then posted to the list.
Lesson 5 Talking and listening about reviews. Writing comparative responses. **Book Week** **There are no set rap activities for this week.**	Although there is no official activity for the rap as it is Book Week, the class work continues. Students collect reviews from the weekend paper and the *Children's Book Council* site to discover the winning titles. Teacher displays awards announcement. Students compare their reviews with judges' comments and with other postings from the email list. They may respond directly to those postings. (NB: this is when the challenge to Simon's opinion occurred, see p. 45). Children could note differences in review writing and features included in comments.
Lesson 6 **Rap Point 3** Do you agree with the judges' choice of the best Picture Book of the Year? Justify your opinion by referring to the reviews posted in Rap Point 2 by your own class or group and other schools.	Individually students decide their personal opinions of the judges' decision. Prepare the outline of a written response in the form of an exposition text. They would need to employ the correct structure for an argument and give clear examples from the text to support their point of view. Students will need to justify their stance referring to the reviews posted in Rap Point 2. In small groups students share their opinions. Then, as a whole class, students discuss the judges' decision. Tally the numbers for and against the judgement, taking note of the key reasons for arguments given.

You may also refer to award reports collected from newspapers during Book Week. Share your ideas and feelings with other rappers.	Post a summary of the results and opinions.
Lesson 7 **Rap Wrap Up** (a) In this rap you have closely examined Picture Books. How has your understanding of a picture book judge's role been developed? (b) What have you enjoyed and learnt from participating in the rap? Post your final response as a short comment.	As a whole class discuss the difficulties of being a book judge (e.g. problems in reaching a consensus) and the considerations judges need to make (e.g. the criteria used to assess picture books). Whole class jointly constructs a paragraph that records their final comments to be posted to the list. Individually students complete a personal evaluation proforma. In small groups share opinions and give feedback to the teacher on the experience of participating in the rap. Recommend future action to be taken. As extension work students could consider designing their own rap to be used with peers or younger children.

Getting started with book raps

Teachers can participate in book raps at different levels of involvement from passive observation to the generation of new raps. It is possible to observe the raps as a silent participant by signing on for the rap but then not sending in any responses. This gives a teacher the chance to see how much commitment is required to be involved in a rap and how the process operates. The next step would be to sign up for a rap and participate in a selection of the rap points as they suit the class programme. It is a common occurrence that schools will sign up, then realize that they do not have the time to complete the rap fully, so they drop out. There is no compunction to complete a rap but if at all possible it is better to complete the rap cycle so that students get a 'taste' of what participation in a rap would involve.

The most fulfilling experience for the teacher and the students is to participate in a full rap by signing on in the beginning and following through all the rap points and accompanying activities as modelled on-line. The rap points set up minimum expectations but it is up to the individual teachers to then develop their own class interpretation of the work needed to form postings. The model given in Box 3.1 of the teacher working with the Book Week rap demonstrated that work could be done ahead of and after the rap.

After participating in existing raps, the next level would be to design your own rap. It is possible, as suggested earlier, to use the basic model of the book rap and organize a rap simply using a school intranet. The teachers of one age group of children could design a rap that suited their literacy goals for the term. The class just down the hall or across the playground could still communicate via email to create an interactive on-line literacy experience for students at a local level.

A challenging level of involvement in a rap would be for a teacher to design a rap her/himself for one of the websites. After one senior primary class had experienced raps several times, they suggested to their teacher that they design a rap for others. They had enjoyed the work and thought they had a good idea of what would make an interesting rap. They chose the age range they wanted to design the rap for, slightly younger than themselves, and the book they wanted to model the rap points on, *Billy the Punk* (Carroll, 1996). They chose that book as they thought it would stimulate good discussion, something they saw as essential for a successful rap. They then designed some thought-provoking rap points that were sent off as a proposal to the http://rite.ed.qut.edu.au/old_oz-teachernet/projects/book-rap/ site. The programming steps found on the site as support structures for potential coordinators were followed (see Figure 3.1). As the rap included rappers emailing the illustrator and posting illustrations to the list, the rap plan was quite complex. The planning of the rap encouraged the students to look closely at the text, and to consider the role of good questions in a learning situation, the importance of planning towards a known literacy outcome and the use of technology as a communication tool.

Conclusion

The raps sites described in this chapter are both established in an Australian context. However, there are many international websites that showcase children talking about books using electronic media. One of these is the Book Chat site from New Zealand (http://english.unitecnology.ac.nz/bookchat/home.html). The format for the discussions on this site is quite similar to the book raps. Another very interesting site is the E-pal site from America (http://www.brick.net/~classact/nbooks.htm). This site includes the potential for children to discuss texts with children who speak a language other than their own. The two web forum discussion sites discussed in Chapter 5 are examples of children's cross-cultural exchange of ideas about books. These include the

Finnish-based *Netlibris*, and the Australian *ELLIE*. There are many other ways that children may interact on-line through a common engagement with literary texts. The next chapter discusses other on-line communities in which students can participate in collaborative co-construction of imaginative narrative.

4 Playing in the MUD, performing in the palace

Introduction

This chapter outlines two different types of on-line communities or 'virtual worlds': a MUD and a palace. These virtual worlds are prolific – hundreds of each type are currently on the net. In each of these hundreds of worlds is a community of participants, who join for pleasure and exist through collaborative participation in community events. Many of the worlds are themed, from social interaction only, to intensive role-playing worlds, which require the people entering into them to adopt various roles for the purpose of playing an interactive on-line 'game'. Whichever the case, the inhabitants of these worlds communicate through a wide range of literate practices. To participate and have a presence in an on-line community is to communicate through multimodal channels – from spoken text, to computer commands, to visual images, to the use of sound effects or sound bytes.

Of most interest in this chapter will be the types of worlds which encourage role-playing, since in these worlds participants are engaged in the collaborative construction of narratives, many of which are based on existing children's literature. Previous research (Dudfield, 1992) examined the heightened use of children's language when participating in role-playing experiences. This research illuminated children's use of more sophisticated texts in terms of vocabulary, adjectival and adverbial clauses and a host of other linguistic features. Other research (Thomas, 2003) has explored the notion that when in on-line spaces, even the act of performing 'one's self' in text (let alone role-playing another character) required high demands of children's language. This chapter will examine the types of literacy required of children when participating in role-playing virtual communities which are based on literature.

In explicating the multiliteracies and literary dimensions of these worlds, many examples are taken from communities that involve people of many age ranges. These are drawn upon to highlight the range of literacy events across the communities. Examples of communities that are devised for children under 16 are also provided, but these are less prolific or are private and restricted to the public for ethical reasons, so fewer examples were found. It is recommended that teachers select one of the existing child-oriented worlds to visit. For teachers with a modest amount of technical knowledge, it is possible to create a palace without too much difficulty. Not for the faint-hearted, creating a MUD requires some programming knowledge and it is recommended that technical assistance be sought for this purpose. We will discuss several suitable existing sites that focus on children's literature both in this chapter and in Chapter 6, however, so minimal technical knowledge is required.

Description of MUD/MOO and examples of its use

MUD is an acronym for multi-user domain or multi-user dungeon. A MUD is a text-based synchronous chat space. A similar type of chat space is called a MOO, MOO being short for MUD, Object-oriented. In these spaces, users log on via a telnetting software program and have the ability to build the atmosphere of the environment by making 'objects' which have particular attributes and which can perform certain functions on command (e.g. an object could be a 'cat', which could be programmed to purr or slink about the room on command). Users need to learn some simple commands to negotiate the space and communicate effectively. If users also wish to make objects, they will need to learn some simple programming language. There are simple commands needed to move from one room to another (e.g. the command 'go south' will transport a user to the room south of the entrance), to view the space and the other players (the command 'look Anya' will result in a screen of information about the player Anya), and to communicate with others (the command from player Iona, 'whisper Anya [hello]' will send Anya a private message saying, 'Iona whispers hello to you').

Traditionally, the boundaries between MUDs and MOOs have been distinct, with MUD environments being dedicated to themed role-playing (traditionally of a Dungeons and Dragons nature), and MOO environments to social interactions. These boundaries have blurred somewhat in recent times, and it is common to find 'role-playing MOOs' as well as social MOOs. We will concentrate on any form of role-playing text-based environment in this chapter, since it is the role-playing that affords children innovative ways of experimenting with narrative. The term MUD will be used throughout, however, we will mean it to also include role-playing MOOs.

There is a wide range of role-playing themed MUDs, from Cyberpunk themes, to ancient Greece themes. Many are devoted to myth, lore and medieval fantasy. Players log on to the space and adopt a character. Some MUDs have a long and complex process for character building. A MUD about Middle

Earth, for example, requires a player to choose between dwarf, hobbit, elf, human, orc, and so on. DartMUD for example (http://www.dartmud.com/) entices players with the lines:

> You may choose to be a gallant warrior, a powerful mage, a wily thief, the best chef in all the land, or any combination of these or other skills. Your character can lust for raw power, work to make the world a more peaceful place, or play the part of a leprous beggar who learns everyone's secrets. You can choose one of fourteen races including some familiar faces, as well as unique races with distinct backgrounds.
> (Dartmud, 2004, on-line)

Players will select a profession and develop skills and talents throughout their participation in various events in the on-line space. As players acquire skills and money, these are included in a player's profile. A profile is partly constructed by the player, and partly by the computer program, which will ascribe it various attributes, skills and rewards that may be gained by the player. A typical character profile might look like the one shown in Figure 4.1. This profile came from a character on the MUD 'Cybersphere', a MUD with a cyberpunk futuristic theme.

Once characters are formed, they begin to participate in the world as that character. Many themed MUDs have associated websites with lists of rules, tips and ideas, maps of the world, and so on, to assist new players in orienting themselves to the world. Experienced players will be marked in various ways to assist new players as they begin their journey into the world. In many communities, these players are called gods or wizards, those this nomenclature alters to fit the theme of the community. Gods and wizards also have additional 'powers' or computer commands at their disposal. These commands include behaviour management commands (i.e. if a player breaches the protocol of the community they can be disconnected and banned) and world-building commands (i.e. some players are able to build new rooms and objects for the world once they have proved their programming skills as well as their trustworthiness).

As players log on to the community, they seek out others and begin role-playing. Sometimes it may take some 'out of character' discussion to negotiate the general focus that the role-playing will take. This strategy is highly recommended when working with children. This will enable the children to have some reflective time to orient themselves before commencing the role-play. Although essential to the community, the role-playing is only one part of belonging to the world, which is built through a rich tapestry of literacy events, including: building a character, creating rooms and objects, thinking of challenges and quests, and elaborating on the myth and lore to provide the contexts for the role-playing.

Fabienne

She's skinny and it makes her look taller than the 5'9" she really is. Her long face isn't exactly beautiful, but it has an intriguing quality. Maybe it's her eyes, her dark eyes that always seem to hide more than they reveal. Or maybe it's her long black hair that hangs around her face as if it's always still wet. Maybe it's her lips, thin but well defined, as if they had been drawn with a very fine pencil. Maybe it's her poise, her back always straight, her head always high. Or maybe it's the way she gesticulates when she speaks, deliberately as if she were conducting a big orchestra. Maybe it's her voice, the kind of voice that would belong to someone with a glass of whisky and a cigarette, sitting in the corner of a dark bar, singing, accompanied by an accordion.

She's wearing a long leather coat. It has a collar of fake raccoon fur that seems to be torn loose from the right lapel. The long leather coat has a double set of buttons that Fabienne keeps unbuttoned. Under her long leather coat you can see the faint glimmer of a burgundy silk shirt. She also wears a faded pair of black jeans. Shiny fourteen hole Dr. Martens cling to her feet.

Fabienne is skilled in Martial Arts, Aikijutsu, Japanese and Gun Repair. Her skills with the knife, swords and pistol are impressive. She has advantages of superhuman intelligence, superior stealth, remarkable strength and dexterity, good thievery and ability to have implants.

She is in excellent health. She is holding a credstick, a katana, a copy of Gideon's Bible and a glass of zot.

Figure 4.1   A character profile created by a member of the Cybersphere MUD community
Source: Dudfield (1999)

Figure 4.2 is an example of role-playing from a gypsy themed MUD in which the players (all older teens) have read and studied a series of literary fiction upon which their world is based.

In this example, the users have researched the Romany language and culture in order to authentically create characters and contexts to role play in a gypsy world. It is on-line experiential drama, with a unique and unparalleled combination of *improvisation* due to the fictional dramatic context, and *reflection* due to the technological medium that allows a degree of delay time and plan out time for 'speech'.

Features evident in this example include: use of explicitly written verbs or processes related to paralinguistic features, bodily movement, facial expressions, and vocal descriptors (e.g. R *walks* over, C *bobs* his head, K *whistles*, R . . . *says*); use of dialogue and punctuation such as . . . to indicate pauses in speech; adverbs (e.g. R . . . nods *faintly*, K . . . turns *slightly*, K says *quietly*) to provide indicators of modality (the degree to which the actions are occurring, e.g. the word quietly tells us that K speaks with a quiet voice, within the possible

K whistles a little to himself as he tends to his garden near the tree. His hands are coated with dirt, but he has not taken off any of his rings.

R walks over near the garden and sets his hands to his waist. "Good evening Kirvo . . ." He turns slightly to C smiling "and prala"

K looks over his shoulder, "Oh . . . greetings, all."

C bobs his head in a nod, smiling crookedly, "Hey there, guys, what's up?"

K hmmms to himself, and says quietly, "I'm trying to sense the relationship between the plants and the spirits of the wind and sky."

R glances over to his tsera and turns back to D "Nothing" C nods faintly, "What, like a dandelion?"

K nods, "Yes prala, exactly." He glances to the tsera a moment, then looks to R, then looks back at his plants.

R raises his brows and sighs as he gazes upon the plants. K keeps looking at the plants, moving soil, "What is it R?"

C has a peek at the vegetation as well, but he isn't a gardener, so his glance isn't with a great deal of understanding.

R lowers his head a little and says "Nothing . . ." He bites his lip a little and changes his tone to speak in Romany.

Figure 4.2   An example of themed role-playing from a gypsy MUD
Source: Dudfield (1998)

range of soft to loud; for a further discussion of modality, see Chapter 1) and adverbials or circumstances describing aspects of the action such as the locations of their physical on-line bodies (e.g. near the tree, near the garden, to his waist, over his shoulder) as cues for each of the other participants. This is a text in progress, a drama unfolding.

User K, who plays the role of the mage gypsy (a 'wise one' or spiritual leader), has interactional control in this small excerpt, but all participants typically have equal degrees of control, offering and using cues to sustain their roles and develop the narrative. A feature of technological literacy is that all participants are able to 'speak' without interruption. As their 'real' or 'ecological' selves are alone at a keyboard, they read, write and respond to the texts on their screen at their own leisure. They have time to reflect and formulate responses. Their words will be processed the instant they press the return or enter key, and will be seen by all. Further discussion of this particular example can be found in Dudfield (1998).

Players sometimes write the stories of their role-playing or the context of their role-playing into myths, which are then published on-line. One example of this is at 'Shattered Kingdoms', see Figure 4.3.

Talde Silvertree lived the first half of his life as a trapper and woodsman in the village of Elisair. He was a quiet and peaceful elf who deeply loved his native forest of Selkwood. However, near the end of his prime, in his hundred and thirty-first summer, shame was brought to the Silvertree name thanks to Talde's actions. He had been accused and convicted by the elders of Elisair of being a drow sympathizer and was outcast from Selkwood. In their shame, Talde, his sister and his cousin left Selkwood, never to return, and travelled to make their home in the woods on the western shores of Lake Everclear.

It was in this forest that Aster was born, many decades later. Aster was the fifth of six children born unto Talde and his wife (little is known about Aster's mother except that she may have been half-elven; Aster does not like to speak about her). Aster lived the first eighty years of her life there, in the forest, with her father, mother, three brothers, two sisters, aunt, uncle, and cousins in a close and independent family. She learned a lot about the ways of the wilds from her father and from the many travellers her family took in who passed through the woods. She heard tales of far away lands and strange creatures which made her young imagination run wild, inspiring her with a lifetime of incurable wanderlust. However, this all came to an end on one cold, rainy night when her father took in the wrong traveller.

Figure 4.3 Example of writing a myth based on role-playing at 'Shattered Kingdoms'
Source: Shattered Kingdoms (2004, on-line)

Another example of writing based on role-playing at a MUD is at 'The Eternal City'. In this case, however, the writing was done as a way of establishing the theme of the MUD in its conception, to provide a context and stimulation for the role-play. A number of myths and legends were written by way of this form of introduction, see Figure 4.4.

The richness of language used in these role-playing texts is, to our minds, both exciting and unique – tapping into and blending what is loved about traditional folk-lore, narrative and storybuilding, with new forms of writing based on the degree of interactivity with others, the type of reflective writing described above and the use of programming commands to perform a range of acts. Children are required to write both as speakers and writers and this combination of orality and writing is something quite unique to internet literacies.

Facilitating knowledge required by teachers for implementing into classroom

Participating in a MUD and navigating inside the worlds require, as previously mentioned, a telnetting program to connect to the space. Many internet

No one remembers who built the Harbor of the Moons, nor its towering counterpart, the spires of unknown stone that rises from the cliffs of Iridine. No one can say when Moonfall first took place, when the first purplish-black storms appeared, roiling through the moonlit countryside in furious silence. No one remembers just how old the inner city really is, nor or to what ends of Midlight its folk were scattered.

Iridine is a vast and ancient metropolis, its origins lost in myth. It is the beloved city of the sun god, Ereal, said to be raised as a monument to his victories over the eclipsing moons. It is home to both the savagery of the great Coliseum and the refinement of the Senate, the twin centers of the mighty Iridine Republic. It is the Eternal City. It always has been and always will be.

The streets of the City course with human life. Legionaries, workers, priests, peddlers, and patricians crowd the plazas and cobblestone roads. Thieves dart amidst the crowds, picking pockets and lifting goods, while constables gallantly attempt to police the busy byways. . . .

Figure 4.4   Example of writing a myth to stimulate role-playing at 'The Eternal City'
Source: Skotos (2004, on-line)

browsers support telnetting protocol automatically, but the interface produced automatically is very rough and raw, and difficult to manage. One problem for example is that when typing in words into the raw telnet program, one cannot see the words until pressing enter. It's important to be able to see what you are typing in a separate line before sending it to the other people in the MUD, for reasons of editing and checking and keeping track of what you are trying to say.

It is best to download a special telnet program which has a much better interface and overcomes this and other problems. Such programs are free on-line and are always being developed and improved by MUD lovers who want to increase their enjoyment and ease of participation. Examples of these include: Gmud and Zmud (for PC users), or MudDweller and MacMush (for Mac users). These can be downloaded free from many sites, for example, the Virginia Tech site managed by Hatfield (2004, on-line), called 'The EBBS Gallery of Client Software for Muds and/or MOOs', which is located at http://ebbs.english.vt.edu/mudmoo.clients.html. Some commercial role-playing and/or interactive gaming MUDs have developed a telnet program with a specially customized graphic interface. An example of this is shown in Figure 4.5.

These examples are from either private or commercially owned MUDS which have been designed by both teens and adults, with access available to anybody. Teachers and parents may want to exercise some caution before allowing their younger children to participate in these communities, as out of

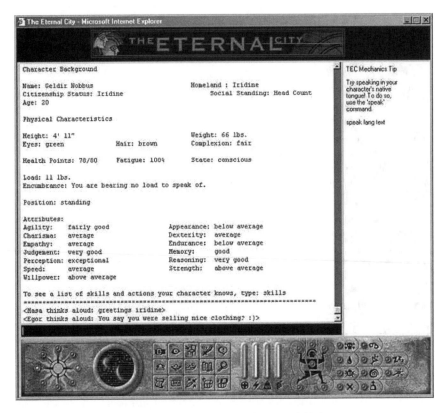

Figure 4.5 An example of a telnet interface from 'The Eternal City'
Source: Skotos (2004, on-line)

character comments could be offensive. Most MUDs have strict rules and protocols and the wizards, gods and administrators ensure a safe environment as best as possible. With some monitoring, most role-playing MUDs would be suitable for older children and teenagers. However, for those who are novices in role-playing or 'MUDDING', or who wish to ensure all other users are either children or teachers, the virtual community of *MOOSE Crossing* is recommended.

MOOSE crossing: a MUD designed for children by children

The most popular MUD-type environment designed for children is Amy Bruckman's Moose Crossing (Bruckman, 1994a, 1994b, 1997). Bruckman has established and developed Moose Crossing over the past eight years with the assistance of both computer designers and educators. Children have participated in the developing of the space as they have developed the necessary programming skills. All members of Moose Crossing are aged 13 and under.

> MOOSE Crossing is an excellent way for kids 13 and under to expand creative writing skills and learn to program at the same time. Kids can create objects ranging from magic carpets to virtual pets to even a pokémon; a world based on your imaginations. They can also build virtual rooms and cities, such as King Tut's Pyramid, the Emerald City of Oz, or Hogwarts. Kids can meet and interact with other kids from all around the world. The world of MOOSE Crossing is built by kids, for kids.
>
> (Bruckman, 1997, on-line)

We will return to discuss MOOSE Crossing later in the chapter.

A rationale for use in pedagogic terms

Understanding the nature of a narrative is a key to purposeful role-playing, in particular, aspects of plot, setting and characterization. In many MUDs, players are also given guidance on how to effectively role-play through text. An emphasis is placed on developing strong characterization and also on understanding aspects about narrative techniques. Casey (2003, on-line) writes, '[r]ole-playing is about characters. More specifically, it's about characterization – making a particular character seem alive, seem real. And even beyond that, we generally want our characters to seem interesting.' Casey explains that one of the important rules for players when developing character is to '*Show, don't tell*' (Casey, 2003, on-line, emphasis in original), and offers the following example:

> Jenny moved through the crowd like a dancer, weaving in and out of the spaces. Her small form slipped easily through places where others could not go, letting her move through where they would be stuck waiting. But the one thing she never did was touch anyone.
>
> (Casey, 2003, on-line)

Typing in the actions and showing various aspects about a character arouse much more curiosity in the readers, and leave questions about the character that the role-playing may unfold. Players are encouraged to type in all of the affectual cues to supply the other players with an understanding of the character's thoughts, emotions and intentions, in order to drive the narrative along. Some experienced players will take a lead role in perpetuating the narrative, by introducing complications and inviting other players to band together on a quest to resolve those complications. Those players with some longevity in games then have stories to boast about and trophies to reveal in future meetings. The participation in a quest will result in the acquisition of some form of social or economic capital that is recognized and valued by the role-playing community.

According to Cucik (2001, on-line) in text-based communities and in particular text-based role-playing adventures, 'the player's brains [are] the most sophisticated graphics device available'. Books have worked on this principle too, but in the virtual MUD world, players need to be able to write vivid descriptions of rooms and actions to help create images in the minds of other players, and this type of descriptive writing is vital for creating the atmosphere of the environment.

A high level of literacy is required for children to effectively participate in on-line communities. For even the simplest form of communication, children need to be involved in a complex process of both writing (to 'speak to others') and reading (to 'read' what other people say to them). In themed role-play spaces, children are also required to use sophisticated vocabulary consistent with both the theme and their role within the role-play. As demonstrated in the example of the gypsy-themed MUD, some children also research other languages to use where appropriate. Also, the need to supply the other players with rich descriptions of actions and emotions results in a highly crafted piece of collaborative writing. Children are motivated to write in various forms for a very strong purpose: the pleasure afforded by the game. MUDs provide meaningful and pleasurable purposes for children to read and write in collaboration with others, the virtual community providing plentiful opportunities for development of literacy skills with a focus on literary texts. Moreover, the computer literacy or 'technoliteracy' skills developed include developing logical understandings and basic programming skills.

As mentioned previously, one of the best MUDs we recommend for teachers of younger children is Amy Bruckman's MOOSE Crossing. Bruckman explains the educational theory behind Moose Crossing, as:

> The design of MOOSE Crossing was guided by the educational theory of constructionism. Constructionism states that we build our own knowledge based on what we experience, and will therefore learn especially well when we build personally meaningful projects. Children on MOOSE Crossing take part in constructing their own projects, which allows them to practice their reading, writing, and programming skills. They are taking part in a hands-on experience which uses their language and programming skills. The MOOSE Crossing community provides ample support for children in the form of a knowledge resource, a sounding board for ideas, and an appreciative audience.
>
> (Bruckman, 1997, on-line)

The wide range of skills children can develop through participation in quests, projects of world-building and interactive role-playing are legion. Through reading and writing in virtual environments, children develop their powers of imagination and inventiveness. Through collaboration with others, they become critically aware of how to manipulate the resources of both language and programming to create their world and participate in the game and role-play. Most importantly, children will be able to participate in the worlds of children's literature through immersing themselves in the characters, plots, and climactic twists of the narrative.

Examples of specific classroom applications

Engaging children in a MUD role-playing experience will require the teacher to prepare some initial off-line classroom activities. Some suggestions for a sequence of lessons are indicated below. These lessons require teachers to locate a suitable MUD and either notify the owner or secure permission from the owner to allow the class to participate. For most g-rated MUDs, permission is required and accounts (which are free of charge) for children to access need to be created by the owner. As noted previously, it is important to go through these steps to ensure children are interacting in a safe space on-line. These lessons are also designed for just one class of children. In the first instance, it is advisable to work with just one class until the teacher and students are all confident with how the MUD works. However, the ideal way for these lessons to be used would be for several interested teachers to all work together in separate classrooms with the off-line work, then join together on the MUD to create a truly interactive role-play, using the affordances of the space to its greatest advantage. Box 4.1 shows the sequence of lessons.

In this sequence of lessons, much work is done off-line to support the on-line work. The teacher needs to scaffold children's understandings carefully throughout the sequence, and the on-line component should be considered as part of the normal literacy programme, not as a replacement for it. We also believe that the work children do on-line should be celebrated off-line, through publishing logs of interactions as a record of their collaborative writing. This could also be valuable in talking to parents about their children's work on-line.

Description of palaces and examples of their use

The palace is a visual virtual world, similar to a MUD but existing through the visual. The palace was an initiative of Jim Baumgartner, who first approached Time-Warner Interactive (a company mostly concerned with role-playing

Box 4.1 MUD role-playing structure

Lesson 1 Reading myths and legends	To prepare children for the types of characters and events which occur in typical MUDs, it is important to first immerse them in the language of myth, legend and folk-lore. During the reading process, the class could make lists of the typical types of characters, and the typical types of quests and events that can be found. Using traditional tales such as the Greek myths and legends, Tolkein's *Lord of the Rings*, or elements from modern tales such as Harry Potter would provide children with an understanding of the language of myths and legends.
Lesson 2 Reading the specific legends of the MUD	In this lesson, the teacher should select the MUD in which children will participate. The teacher should collect all of the background myths, legends and character guides to read through and discuss with children. The teacher should guide children in their understandings that myths and legends have both heroic 'good' characters, and not so heroic 'unseemly' characters, and that myths and legends only work because their characteristic feature is quest to overcome evil.

Lesson 3
Writing and drawing character descriptions based on a theme
	Children select characters and decide on the features of the character to fit within the theme of the MUD. There should be a range of both good and unseemly, and the teacher may like to remind children of the features of good descriptions (e.g. adjectival and adverbial phrases to build up an image of what the character looks like and how it acts and moves).
	    Children can also draw their character and consider the visual features which will highlight their inner character as well as their outward appearance. They should use resources of visual grammar to assist in their drawings, for example 'my character has shifty eyes, he never makes a direct contact (or "demand") by gazing out at the audience because he doesn't want anybody to discover his secrets' (Chapter 1 outlines the scope of visual grammar elements that may be used here).
	    Students should share their descriptions and drawings. These could be placed on a display board for the duration of the series of lessons, so that the class can read and discuss them when off-line.

	Children can then log onto the MUD for the first time and be guided in writing their character descriptions on-line into the MUD space.
Lesson 4 Storytelling about characters	Children should write their own legend to describe the history of their own character. This is particularly important because it will provide motivations for actions, behaviours and events to come. For those less seemly characters, it will also reveal what happened to them or their ancestors to cause them to be unseemly. These can be published on-line or published within the MUD (on the MUD message boards) for all to read. Teachers may also like to make a hard copy book of 'Our myths and legends'.
Lesson 5 Learning how to emote: basic commands	All MUDs will have a list of commands and an associated help file to assist new users in basic movement about the MUD into different rooms, and in ways to communicate to the other users. MUDs vary in the commands they use, but one example is the 'whisper' command. The command, ***whisper <user> hello***, will send a private 'whisper' or message to the user saying hello. The specific user and no others in the room only see this message. The teacher and children can explore and experiment in this lesson, practising the commands and looking at the help files to learn how to move about. The teacher may like to print the help files for children to read when off-line, but this play or exploratory time is crucial in helping children develop the confidence of using the space effectively before commencing the role-play.
Lesson 6 Beginning the role-play in character	Children should now be ready to begin the role-playing in character. The teacher should ask the children to log on and pretend it is just another normal day in their character's lives. It may be advisable to start groups of children in different rooms doing particular tasks (for instance, one group might be in the 'market' space, purchasing goods and another group might be in the village square, talking to each other about their morning). Children should be encouraged to move about the world and mix with different groups in role. The teacher could keep a log of all the interactions to talk about with the class off-line, using a range of questions as a guide such as:

- What were the actions that Bethany did and what did they tell us about her character? (The children could highlight the verbs or processes used by Bethany.)
- How did Laura's description of the way she moved in the room show something about her character? (The children could highlight adverbs and adjectives used by Laura.)
- What did the descriptions Adam used to portray the emotions on his face tell us about he was feeling? (The children could search for Adam's use of sensing verbs (mental processes) or adjectives used to describe his facial features.)
- How did Joel show us that he was an unpleasant character? (The children could search through Joel's contributions and identify the type of language he used to create a negative impression of him. If the children have done work on evaluative language or appraisal (see Droga and Humphrey (2002) for a simple introduction to appraisal), then they could be asked specifically to identify the words of negative 'affect' used by Joel).

Through this guided reading of the role-playing log, the teacher is scaffolding the children's understandings of the types of language to suit both the theme of the MUD and the affordances of the on-line environment. The teacher is also making explicit to children the grammatical resources used by authors to construct characterizations in their narratives.

Lesson 7 Developing the role-play: introducing a complication	Off-line, the class could discuss an appropriate complication to introduce into the role-play. It could be based on what has happened in the role-playing to date (a review of the logs might help in deciding the complication), or it could be based on ideas taken from existing myths and legends but adapted to the theme of the MUD. A discussion off-line will provide some time for rehearsal of general ideas and provide a scaffold for their storying on-line. When ready, the children can go on-line and perform the role-play. This may take more than one lesson if it is working well. Once again the teacher can make a log of the interaction for off-line reflection and discussion. The log

	could be displayed for the period between lessons 7 and 8 to give children opportunities to consider how the complication might be resolved.
Lesson 8 Resolving the complication (denouement)	Using the written transcripts or 'logs' of the role-play (which can be obtained by activating the 'log' function, this will automatically create a text file which will record the role-play), the teacher can brainstorm with the class the ways in which the complication could be resolved. It may be that different groups could devise alternative resolutions. When some ideas are agreed upon, the children could log on and complete the role-play, either with one or multiple resolutions.
Lesson 9 Making storyboards	In this lesson, children have an opportunity to retell their own version of the role-play, focusing on how their character acted, felt, and interacted. Children can make a storyboard to illustrate their story from beginning to end, telling it from their point of view. In creating the images, children should carefully consider the relationships between themselves and others, as well as the way in which they want their character to be perceived by the readers of their storyboard. They should once again draw upon their understanding of the grammatical resources used to create meaning.
	In creating the dialogue, children may like to make use of the actual dialogue from the role-playing logs. If their character wasn't involved in any speaking for a particular scene, they should be encouraged to use thought bubbles to reveal what their character was thinking. Children should also include directions to specify action, movement and emotion for each scene on the storyboard. This could be taken from the role-play logs but could also be developed or altered to show a particular character's perspective more clearly.
Lesson 10 Sharing and reflection	This lesson should be a celebration of the sequence of lessons, where children share their storyboards as well as their thoughts about the work they have done. During reflection, the teacher could guide discussion using questions such as:
	• What did you learn in these lessons? • What did you learn about myths and legends?

- What did you learn about the ways in which authors construct characters?
- What did you learn about writing a storyboard?
- What did you learn about the ways in which illustrators construct characters?
- What did you think the most important part of the role-play was and why?
- What were some of the things you learned about computer programming?
- What parts of the sequence of the lesson did you enjoy most and why do you think that was?

computer games) with his conceptualization, and after some development was taken over by Electric Communities. Baumgartner and Electric Communities wanted to create a world that resembled an interactive cartoon, deliberately choosing not to create a photo-realistic world, in order for the palace to create a sensory aesthetic with wide appeal.

A room in a palace somewhat resembles a comic book backdrop in which the characters can create their own narratives, whether they be simply conversational, confessional, theatrical, soap opera, educational, or other. The palace has many rooms: some of these are connected in theme, others discrete. Figure 4.6 shows the entrance room for the palace 'Kids, Enfants, Kinder' (Thomas, 1999–2003, on-line).

An avatar is the visual image used to represent a participant in the visual world. There are many styles of avatars available, from sultry looking models, to animé cartoon figures, or other objects such as a cloud. Each participant has a virtual wardrobe of avatars and costumes to select from, including a range of accessories such as glasses and hats. Here most of the avatars are cartoonish-style children; the avatar of the realistic-looking person is the adult teacher working with the group of children. Each participant has avatars available to represent a range of poses, such as standing, leaning, sitting, stretching and dancing. Some participants swap and change avatars more than a hundred times in an hour, others will select their favourite avatar and never change.

The range of palaces on-line is varied and similar to MUDs: from role-playing worlds, to spaces of social interaction. Media companies have been quick to develop their own palaces for various purposes. In the months leading up to the premiere of the movie *The Blair Witch Project* (Sanchez and Myrick, 1999), a *Blair Witch* palace was established to help create interest and intrigue in the story. The station producing the TV show *South Park* (Parker, 1997–2004), set up a palace for fans of the show, and the executive producer of the show, Trey Parker, visited on several occasions to interact with fans.

Figure 4.6   Entrance room to the 'Kids, Enfants, Kinder' palace
Source: Thomas (1999–2003, on-line)

There are other fan-based palaces (some volunteer, others commercial), which encourage the writing of 'fan fiction'. Fan fiction is a term used to describe the narratives created by fans to write possible episodes of their favourite TV shows. This phenomenon is broad-based and certainly not restricted to the palace, however, on the palace fans can both write their episode, then adopt their favourite characters and organize virtual performances of their scripts. The *Galaxy Station* palace (palace://thegalaxystation. com:9998), for example, encourages the writing and performing of *Star Wars* fan fiction. Similarly, there are palaces dedicated to other movie favourites such as the palace Emerald City (palace://oz.chatn.net:9998), which is dedicated to the Wizard of Oz. A number of palaces have been established as sites for learning as well as entertainment, some by educators, some by parents, but most by the young people who inhabit these spaces for specific purposes that will be described below.

Some teachers have been using palaces as a resource for teaching communication skills, internet literacy, graphic design, collaborative storytelling. In 2000, Swiss educator Edgar Goetschi won a European 'Netdays' award for his teaching program using the palace. On his palace, named *MeetPoint* (Goetschi, 1999–2004, on-line), Goetschi has images from many different countries as different room backgrounds, and uses them to immerse children in the culture and festivities of other countries. The Italian room is an image of Venice, and upon entrance, children's avatars are automatically turned into a mask, and they share information about the carnival of Venice, for example. He also has avatar contests, with children choosing a theme and designing appropriate avatars using their graphic programs, and then parading themselves (and their hard work!) in front of other student judges. Goetschi includes images of the school building and of Switzerland for their friends from other countries to learn about their culture. Although the main language in Switzerland is German, children also learn French as a second language. Goetschi has a Paris room and only French is permitted to be spoken in that room.

Other volunteer palaces have been designed for a range of educational purposes. *Kids Chat* is a palace developed by a group of US parents who wanted to ensure their children had opportunities to participate in safe communities on-line. One of the features of this palace was the way in which children could post questions about any schoolwork they were experiencing difficulty with. Parents organized volunteer tutors to come on-line and provide additional support for those children. Kids Chat also held trivia nights, quiz nights and other fun competitions as a part of the regular community social events. The *Scout Hut* is a palace designed by parents and scout leaders to teach scouting principles. The *Job Shop* palace is a free job search workplace palace, holding regular tutorials such as 'how to perform well in an interview'. Other examples of palaces based purely on children's literature are discussed in Chapter 6.

However, educators and parents make up only a small proportion of the palaces dedicated to teaching and learning. Young people themselves design by far the majority of palaces with an educational purpose, to teach others how to participate in the palace effectively. These palaces hold regular lessons on various elements of computer graphics (e.g. how to make your own avatar, how to work with colour palettes in your graphic program, how to make animated room backgrounds) and various elements of programming (e.g. how to make objects move about on the screen, how to include pop-up text, and so on).

Using palaces in educational contexts

Over the past decade, society has embraced a 'visual turn' (Jay, 1989: 49), or a 'pictorial turn' (Mitchell, 1994: 13), and is now more than ever seen as 'a society of the spectacle' (Debord [1967] 1977), in which imagery is central to the creation of identity and the gathering and distribution of knowledge (Chaplin, 1994). Visual culture and visual research methodology have exploded in the literature (Abbott, 2002; Berger 1972, 2003; Jenks, 1995; Mirzoeff, 2001; Norris, 2002; Prosser, 2001). There can be little doubt that the visual worlds of cyberspace reflect this 'cultural turn' (Harvey, 1989) of visual saturation. This is especially so since 1992, when Tim Berners-Lee and Marc Andreeson invented the GUI (graphical user interface) turning our computer screens from green text to thousands of colours, and adding iconography and images.

Lemke (1998) claims that multimedia authoring and reading skills will become the generic literacies of the Information Age. He argues that educators need to help students develop the technical, critical and analytical skills to become successful readers of hypertexts, decoders of the visual and analysts of the text as a pastiche. They must develop the ability to read images, navigate and achieve a sense of text, and have an understanding of the representational codes and multilogues, which are used so profusely in cyberliteracies. Kress and van Leeuwen (1996) insist that 'visual literacy' will become an essential tool.

Landow (1998) highlights the way in which texts are now co-authored in collaborative interactive exchanges within cyberculture. He argues that the notion of a single author of a text has become outdated. He explains:

> By actively engaging themselves in the continuous exchange and proliferation of collectively-generated electronic publications, individually-designed creative works, manifestos, live on-line readings, multi-media interactive hypertexts, conferences, etc., Avant-Pop artists and the alternative networks they are part of will eat away at the conventional relics of a bygone era where the individual artist-author creates their beautifully-crafted, original works of art to be consumed primarily by the elitist art-world and their business-cronies who pass judgement on what is appropriate and what is not.
>
> (Landow, 1998, on-line)

According to Landow, collaboration, collective writing, collective artistry and group dynamics have become an integral part of social practices on-line. The classroom example included below reflects Landow's ideas and is a good example of the ways in which children are actively and co-operatively creating a blend of old and new forms of narrative in on-line spaces.

Setting up the palace

Some palaces have been designed so that they can be accessed from inside a web browser. Details of one example of this are discussed in Chapter 6. Accessing the palace through a web browser, however, does not allow all the features of the palace to be activated, so we recommend teachers download the free *Palace User* software. If teachers wish to explore all palaces available, the free software can be located at the *Palace Planet* website (http://www.palaceplanet.net). If teachers want access to a limited number of G-rated palaces only, then the software can be downloaded from the ELLIE website (Thomas, 2002–2005). The specialized software is recommended because it has features which can be customized by each user, including: the *avatar and props* and the *cyborg script*. Once downloaded, we recommend teachers explore these features.

The *avatar and props bag* holds the avatars, images used to represent the user when on the palace, as well as the props, which can be attached to the user. A prop is an object that can be worn near or placed over the face; or a small object that can be held (like a baseball bat or a cup) or attached (like a hat, a pair of sunglasses or a wig). Avatars and props can be found in various palace 'libraries' of images, but can also be home-made, from photos or images preferred by the user. A picture of a child's cat, for example, could be turned into a prop, and then be seemingly sitting with the child, as part of the child's avatar. Avatars and props can be animated, so, using the same example of the cat, the cat's tongue could be animated to drink from a saucer of milk, or its head could turn backwards and forwards as if to survey the room.

The cyborg script (denoted as the cyborg.ipt file in the user's Palace folder) allows each user to create fun words, actions, sounds and/or images to appear or disappear on command. Typing in the word 'party', for example, might then execute the associated script from the cyborg file to produce images (props) of balloons, streamers, confetti, flowers, and so forth, all about the room. Libraries of cyborg scripts are attainable at palaces and on palace help websites such as the one at *Palace Planet* as mentioned above. There, users can pick and choose ready-made scripts for their cyborgs, as well as coding their own.

One final point to make about the palace environment is that it allows for different levels of users to be denoted, those of member, wizard and god. At most palaces, a member may enter, enjoy the environment, execute cyborg scripts, and participate in the community. A wizard, on the other hand, has access to special 'powers', that is, special, wizard-only commands. These commands include those used for regulatory purposes (such as kick <username>, which would allow the wizard to enforce any member violating the rules of agreed code of conduct or netiquette to exit the community), and those used for building purposes and coding purposes (such as createroom <name of room>, which would allow the wizard to make new rooms for the palace at will). It is recommended that some responsible children be given opportunities to be wizards, though this will be at the discretion of the owner of the palace.

Learning about role-playing

Teachers wanting to have children role-playing on the palace should show children an example of a role-play and discuss its features. Role-playing on the palace is a little different to the example shown earlier in the chapter related to role-playing on a MUD. Figure 4.7 illustrates a sample role-playing session between two characters, Maltriel and Eomer, at the Middle Earth palace (Sorenson, 2000–2005). More information about the Middle Earth palace is

---

Eomer: *ignores the hurt welling up from her repeated insults and just nods*

Maltriel: *she walks into her room . . . sighing . . . . back to her prison, though it may be fair and wishes that the rider upon his fell beast had seen her, and taken her back to the mordor army camp, where she would be with angmar most dear once again*

Eomer: *Eomer stands at the door, hating the moment of leaving his sister, though she does not recognize him.*

Eomer: *He wishes to embrace her and tell her of his affection for her, how much he missed her when she was thought dead*

Eomer: *but he knows she considers him an enemy*

Maltriel: *she wonders why the king stands in her doorway, lingering for so long*

Eomer: *He smiles politely and bids her farewell*

Eomer: *A guard closes the door*

Maltriel: your majesty . . .? *she asks*

Maltriel: aanug zark, skakh izub *she calls back to eomer*

Eomer: *Eomer opens the door again when she calls*

Eomer: Lady, you know I cannot understand the Black Speech.

Eomer: What did you say?

Maltriel: oh . . . forgive me then. i said, 'good day, my lord.'

Eomer: *smiles broadly and bows* Good day, my lady.

Eomer: *He closes the door again*

Eomer: *but lingers outside it taking deep breaths to compose himself*

Eomer: *He reassures himself that someday the spell will be broken and she will recognize him as her brother*

Maltriel: *she goes back to her bed and lies down, feeling weak again . . . the actions of her enemies confuse her . . . she had been told they were evil, and they were cowards . . . but they seem polite and kind to her.

Maltriel: *she only hopes it is not because she is a woman, do they treat her so.*

Figure 4.7 An example of a role-play at the Middle Earth palace
Source: Sorenson (2000–2005)

included in Chapter 6. In the role-play, participants use an asterisk (*) to denote the actions they are involved in to distinguish it from speech.

In this role-play, the participants have imagined an alternative ending to *Lord of the Rings: The Return of the King* (Tolkien, 1955), one in which the evil Sauron had the ring, and had kidnapped and brainwashed Eowyn to think her name is Maltriel and to believe that she fights for Mordor. This is an ongoing role-play run by several of the members of the Middle Earth virtual community, and records of the role-play are kept on one of the member's (The Quiet Wraith) websites (http://members.aol.com/thequietwraith/). Teachers could use examples such as the one in Figure 4.7 as well as ones from this website to identify the features of the role-playing such as the combination of dialogue between characters and the actions written inside the asterisks to drive the narrative forward. Other features of role-playing are similar to those discussed in relation to the gypsy MUD role-play outlined in Figure 4.2.

Examples of specific classroom applications

The palace *Kids, Enfants, Kinder* was established by Angela Thomas in 1999 to explore children's virtual role-playing and collaborative storying. Children from Australia, Canada, the USA, Switzerland and France participated over two years in a range of interactive on-line experiences. One of the most popular features of this palace was the virtual theatre performances of Greek mythology. In particular, the children enjoyed reading and participating in the myth 'Persephone's Story'. Figure 4.8 is the first 'room' introducing the myth.

This is the myth about Demeter, goddess of nature, and her daughter Persephone who was kidnapped by Hades and taken down to the Underworld. To participate in this story, children first read through an on-line animated version of the legend (this was built into the palace) to the point in the story where Demeter cursed the land and the earth became barren. At this stage, children were invited to select a character from a range shown in a book (see Figure 4.9). Clicking on the character's name would provide background information for the character. Clicking the image would automatically turn the avatar into that character.

The role-playing varied considerably from group to group but mainly consisted of the characters bemoaning the plight caused by the devastation of Demeter's curse. Usually the teacher (or an assigned child) would enter in role as Demeter (who would refuse to take away the curse until Persephone had been returned safely from the Underworld), and then Hades (who would refuse to allow Persephone to return), followed by the village mayor (who would urge the villagers to make a plan to kidnap Persephone back from the Underworld). Various students were allocated tasks to find out about the Underworld and various other Greek characters.

Figure 4.8 The space for the beginning of the role-play about Persephone and Demeter
Source: Thomas (1999–2003, on-line)

The next part of the virtual drama involved the children (villagers) in the whiteboard room drawing a map and telling of the folklore and family stories they had 'heard' about the perilous journey from their village into the Underworld. Figure 4.10 shows the map in progress, with Cerberus, the three-headed hound, guarding the entrance to the Underworld, the poisonous attacking squids of the River Styx, the frightening pecking parrots, the evil pit of snakes, and so on. Each 'villager' was asked to draw or add something on to the map, and to tell the story related to their drawing or addition. Some groups of children then made special items to assist the brave volunteers who were to rescue Persephone.

These special items included, for example, pictures done with graphic programs of nets, bottles of potions, special armour for their characters to wear (which was converted into an avatar so it could actually be 'worn'), and different types of texts, such as lyrics to a song which would soothe savage Cerberus,

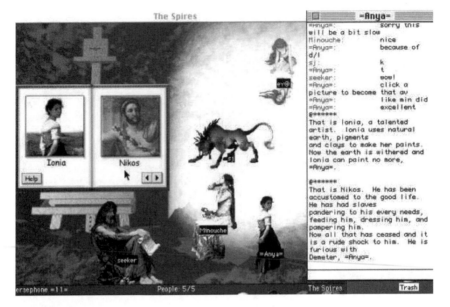

Figure 4.9 Participants select their role character
Source: Thomas (1999–2003, on-line)

prayers using respectful language to Zeus to ask for help, spells to 'freeze' the snakes or to turn them into stone, and so on.

The role-play would conclude with Persephone and the volunteer rescuers successfully returning from the Underworld to recount their perilous journey, explaining how they had escaped and survived, as well as answering villagers' questions. Students then had a chance to reflect out of role and to publish any of the writing they had created throughout the drama, such as their imaginary folk tales or their songs. Teachers reported back on the enthusiasm of students and the high quality of writing and graphic designs that were produced.

Conclusion

Children have embraced the affordances of technological advances in cyberspace. According to the Australian Bureau of Statistics (2003, on-line) in the 2000 census, 45 per cent of Australian households with children under the age of 18 had internet access. Of children between 5 and 14, 51 per cent used the internet for chatroom purposes, an equal number of males and females fell into this category, and there was no apparent difference between the proportion of children using the internet in the city compared to those using it in the country (Australian Bureau of Statistics, 2000). Based on the exponential

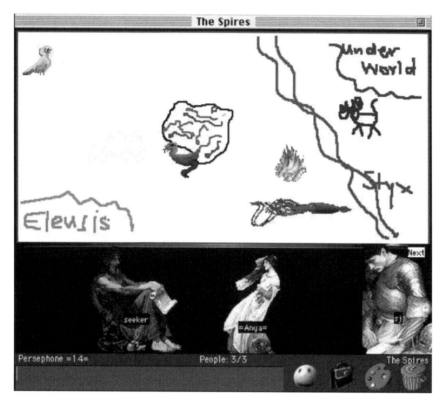

Figure 4.10   Participants create a map of the journey to the Underworld
Source: Thomas (1999–2003, on-line)

growth of internet usage in the past and projected figures by the ABS, it is likely that use by children under 18 (in the Australian context) will rapidly increase. Australia is but one of the Western countries with a high internet usage by children. According to a report commissioned by the US census (Newburger, 2000), in the year 2000, approximately 30 per cent of all children between 3 and 17 in the USA had (and used) the internet at home. As increasingly more children come on-line and participate in on-line spaces, teachers would be wise to explore and exploit these spaces to provide both safe and positive learning experiences for children.

Advocates of digital media argue that the internet, due to its open, global nature, allows children freedom from adult control, to escape from the usual boundaries and lines between childhood and adulthood, and to define themselves in alternative ways from their off-line selves. Katz (1997) argues that the ways in which children are creating their own autonomous cultures and communities is one way children are bringing about new forms of cultural expression. In cyberspace, children have the potential to become more active and participatory through their involvement in virtual communities. If they do, and how they might do it, are central concerns for society.

In this chapter we have argued that MUDs and palaces are exciting on-line spaces for the construction of new types of blended narrative and storying. They offer opportunities for children to develop expertise in communication and electronic literacies, graphic design, computer programming, collaborative storytelling, understanding children's literature, collaborative problem solving and in becoming responsible members of a community.

5 A snapshot of three teachers' classroom practices integrating ICT and children's literature

Introduction

In this chapter we illustrate the work of three teachers: Jenny, Mark and Coco, as they integrate and make use of the affordances of information and communication technologies in their classroom practices. These teachers have worked to varying degrees over the past five to ten years integrating the use of computers into their classroom practices, and their work reflects their wealth of experiences over this time. Additionally, it reflects their considered experimentation and exploration of the possibilities and potentials of using ICTs in the classroom in meaningful ways, to enrich and enhance their literacy programmes.

The snapshot of Jenny's classroom illustrates a teacher beginning to include websites to enrich literature-based units of work that have a focus on visual literacy and narrative structures, putting into practice some of the ideas outlined previously in Chapters 1 and 2. Her unit of work described in this chapter is designed particularly for younger children aged 7 to 9. The snapshot of Mark's classroom reflects his efforts to engage his class in which many of the children have English as a second language, in interactions with children from Finland. He worked with the authors on a project called ELLIE (Electronic Literature and Literacies in International Education) to explore the use of electronic forums to excite and stimulate children's discussions about books and e-books. The use of forums to talk about books is discussed in Chapter 3, in terms of what some teachers call 'book raps'. Mark had not explored electronic literature prior to working on the ELLIE project, so he was excited to introduce this new concept to children, and extremely impressed with children's responses to the unit of work he implemented. Coco's snapshot represents a teacher with an interest in developing her children's collaborative narrative writing using the on-line virtual environment of the palace as a stimulus. The palace was discussed in Chapter 4.

Through sharing these stories and explicit examples of lessons implemented by the three teachers, we present a range of exemplars for the integration of ICT and children's literature in the literacy classroom. As Snyder and Joyce (1998) asserted, not to attend to the possibilities of new technologies would be a considerable neglect of duty.

Snapshot 1: Jenny

Jenny has been developing her work with both children and teachers in the area of visual literacy. Working as both a teacher and a literacy advisor with teachers, she has developed an interest in enhancing her work with children and teachers by exploring ways to integrate the use of ICTs with her work on visual literacy. Here she shares her unit of work with younger children using websites related to children's literature, coupled with a movie version of a children's book. As Margaret Mackey (2002) has noted, we are living in an age of multiple versions of texts. In this unit about *Shrek*, Jenny shows how she encourages young children to explore websites, movies and original versions of a narrative, see Box 5.1.

Box 5.1   Unit of work for young children: *Shrek*

Background information about the texts	This unit for 7 to 9-year-old children is based on the picture book *Shrek* by William Steig (1990) and the Dreamworks movie adaptation of the story. The movie internet site www.shrek.com is also used as a resource. In the picture book, Shrek overcomes a number of perils on his way to find his princess. However, the traditional narrative phrasing is given a 'monster' twist. His parents 'kicked' him goodbye instead of 'kissed' him goodbye, and the happy couple live 'horribly' ever after instead of 'happily' ever after.
	The images in the book are 'long shots' showing the characters from an impersonal distance and through drawings that have low modality, intentionally not depicting the characters as realistic. In contrast, the movie version has complex images that appear very close to realistic and the viewer sees the characters from a variety of social distances including intimate views. The plot of the movie varies significantly from the original story with many more characters, including several

	from well-known fairytales and with additional complexities of plot that a movie-length story allows. Both versions highlight the message, 'Be yourself'. The unit of work explores the structure of narrative texts and visual and verbal narrative techniques.
Lesson 1 Comparison of versions of the story	• Whole-class discussion about *Shrek* the movie, children share their opinions about favourite characters and the theme of the story. • The teacher appoints willing children to go in role as the characters in the movie and participate in 'Hot Seat', answering questions posed by classmates about their character. (Hot Seat is a drama technique whereby one child enters a selected role, sits in the 'hot seat' as a symbol for the role-playing to commence, and responds to questions in character. It is always valuable to brainstorm the questions that the children may like to find out about the character to give the 'hot seat' children a little time to think about how they might answer. The teacher should be the first person to be 'hot seated' to provide a model for appropriately responding to questions if children are new to this technique.) • In small groups children complete a chart briefly outlining the plot, listing the characters and describing the theme of the movie. • The teacher reads the picture book to the class and leads a discussion of the plot, characters and theme, comparing them to the movie version of the story. The class jointly constructs a chart to display on the wall with those created by small groups.
Lesson 2 Exploration of movie site www.shrek.com	• Whole class uses the computer lab to explore www.shrek.com, with a particular focus on the character descriptions and images. The teacher may provide a 'viewing guide' to scaffold children's purposeful viewing of the images, including such questions as: 'What colours are used for each of the characters?', 'What has the illustrator done to show the difference between

	the heroes and the villains of the story?', 'What parts of each character seem to be the most carefully drawn?', and so on.
	• Once the class is back in the classroom, the teacher leads a discussion of the images in *Shrek* the movie comparing them to the illustrations in the picture book.
Lesson 3 Noun groups	• The teacher revises the discussion about images from the last lesson.
	• Using copies of screen shots from shrek.com on the data projector or overhead projector, the teacher defines 'noun groups' and uses an example from the character descriptions on-line to highlight the use of adjectives and adjectival phrases to develop the noun group, for example: 'Lord Farquaad, the measly four-foot-tall ruler of Duloc', 'the neat, orderly and power-hungry Lord Farquaad'. The teacher could then take one of the given descriptions and demonstrate to children how to turn that description into a noun group, for example, in the character profile on Dragon, we read: 'it breathes fire and eliminates knights'. The teacher could show children how to change this into: 'the fire-breathing, knight-eliminating dragon', and so on.
	• The class contribute to jointly writing descriptions of another character and the teacher encourages the use of appropriate and effective noun groups.
	• The class break into small groups and use paper copies of screen shot images to write further descriptions.
	• The teacher displays modelled, joint and independently constructed descriptions on a wall in the classroom, highlighting the children's effective selection of noun groups.
Lesson 4 Narrative structure, story maps	• The teacher models the creation of a story map of a well-known fairytale or recently shared story.
	• In small groups, children create two story maps showing both the movie and picture book stories of *Shrek*.
	• Discuss and compare story maps, as a class.

Lessons 5 and 6
Rotating groups –
narrative techniques

- The teacher defines 'Given' and 'New' (see Chapter 1 – 'Compositional Meanings') and gives examples using images from texts known to the whole class. The teacher then gives an explanation of the activities and assigns each group a task. Children will complete two activities in Lesson 5 and another two in Lesson 6. The teacher will supervise all groups but gives focused attention to activity one.
  1. Children view part of the movie *Shrek* and comment on the use of Given and New with assistance from the teacher. (The movie shows Shrek and the donkey walking from left to right across the screen as they journey to rescue the princess and as they return the layout is reversed.)
  2. Children use a worksheet (see Figure 5.1) to guide their observations and comment on the

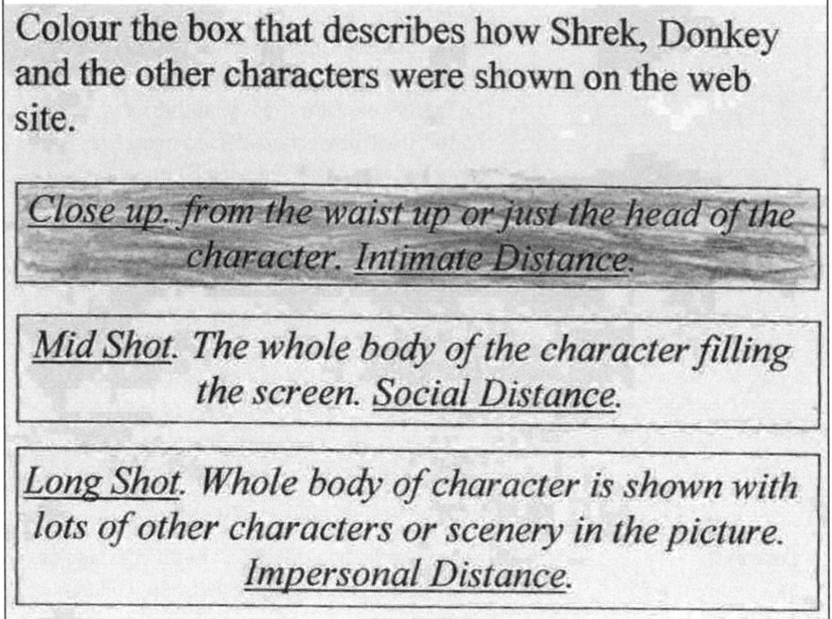

Colour the box that describes how Shrek, Donkey and the other characters were shown on the web site.

Close up. from the waist up or just the head of the character. Intimate Distance.

Mid Shot. The whole body of the character filling the screen. Social Distance.

Long Shot. Whole body of character is shown with lots of other characters or scenery in the picture. Impersonal Distance.

Figure 5.1 Example of worksheet for visual literacy activity

	use of close up/intimate distance shots on www.shrek.com.
	3. Children use multiple copies of the picture book to find and record all of the noun groups in the text.
	4. Children read from a collection of fractured fairytales/stories with fairytale references. For example, *The Frog Prince Continued* by Jon Scieszka and Steve Johnson (1991) and *The Stinky Cheese Man and Other Fairly Stupid Tales* by Jon Scieszka and Lane Smith (1992).
Lesson 7 Intertextuality and Fractured Fairytales	• The teacher leads a discussion about the fractured fairytales read in Lessons 5 and 6 sharing some stories in part or whole. • Children make lists of the original fairytales referred to in the fractured versions or the traditional characters mentioned. • The whole class watches the ending of the *Shrek* movie where fairytale characters join Shrek and Donkey in karaoke. Children list the fairytale creatures present. • The teacher explains the way authors and movie creators use known characters to make the viewer feel like they have been let in on a secret, thus engaging the viewer.
Lesson 8 Modelled writing	• The whole class use the computer lab to explore a number of websites showing fractured fairytales, e.g. *The True Story of The Three Little Pigs* at www.shol.com/agita/pigs.htm and Roald Dahl's fractured version of a number of fairytales at www.cupola.com/html/wordplay/htm • Once back in the classroom, the teacher models the creation of her own fractured tale drawing attention to the narrative structure.
Lesson 9 Independent writing, narrative	• The teacher leads a discussion of the message of both versions of *Shrek* and elicits from children that the theme 'don't be afraid to be yourself' is portrayed through both stories. • The teacher reviews the modelled fractured fairytale from last lesson.

- Children are asked to create their own fractured fairytale, which contains a message such as the one in *Shrek*. This lesson serves as an assessment of children's understanding of the concepts taught through this unit of work.

Classroom considerations

The classroom was set up with two computers connected to the internet, a television and video, a copy of *Shrek* on video, three copies of the picture book and other picture books with fairytale references. The video of the *Shrek* movie was available for children to watch at school outside of class time or to borrow and view at home prior to the unit of work. Children were placed in mixed ability groups for group work.

Snapshot 2: Mark

Mark is a teacher in the western suburbs of Sydney, Australia. He works in a school where over three-quarters of the children speak English as a second language. Mark works part-time on a class of 10–11-year-old children and also has a part-time position as the school's computer advisor. Mark had worked for some years with his classes using a range of software with children, including the use of Powerpoint for the presentation of group and individual class projects, and the use of graphic programs to create digital art. He used the internet as a source for researching information for school projects, but was looking for meaningful ways for children to use the interactive possibilities of the medium. Mark joined the 'Electronic Literature and Literacies in International Education project' (ELLIE) being conducted by the authors of this book, and worked closely with support and advice from Jennifer Asha in his classroom, to explore these possibilities with his students.

The ELLIE project was conducted in two phases. In the first phase we organized Mark's class to interact with a class of children in Finland, using the Finnish site called *Netlibris* (http://www.netlibris.net/international/). Netlibris was designed by Finnish educators Minttu Ollila and Teresa Volotinen in 1996 to enrich teacher's programs in children's literature. The original Finnish project, entitled *Matilda*, had as its aims the following:

- combine cooperative learning and individual curriculum in distance learning;
- design and organize an ICT project that appeals particularly to girls;
- cooperation in offering the top students individual curriculum and expert tutoring;

- encourage and challenge the good readers
  - to read more and different books
  - to share their reading experience with other book lovers;
- increase reading among other students by using the Matilda students' resources at classroom and school level;
- have students as responsible and empowered owners of the project: in choosing the literature, setting the goals, designing the activities and in evaluating the process.

(Netlibris, 1996–2005, on-line)

This project was extremely successful, winning many local and international awards for excellence in the use of ICT in the classroom and learning. Consequently, the site has flourished and grown beyond Finland and is now an international program where teachers and children all over the world talk about children's literature. More about Netlibris and its aims can be found at both the Netlibris website (1996–2005, on-line) or from an article published by Miller (2000).

Through this site, Mark organized for his class of children to work with a class of children in Espoo, Finland. After much email discussion between Mark, the Finnish teachers, and the ELLIE project team, it was decided that the children would read the David Almond novel *Skellig* (Almond, 1998) as the first stage of the project. This award-winning novel was popular with both the Finnish and Australian audiences and was accessible in both English and Finnish, so was an excellent choice.

Mark worked with the ELLIE team and his class of children to explore the novel *Skellig*. In particular, they explored ways in which David Almond and the illustrator of the front cover of the novel used image and text to construct meaning. Mark, the Finnish teachers and the ELLIE team worked collaboratively on this sequence of lessons. As children in each class learnt progressively more about the novel, they were encouraged to write their thoughts in a formal response to the text, post it to Netlibris, and interact with the ideas posted by other children. This interaction occurred in a similar manner to the book raps as described in Chapter 3. Children responded to the novel and shared their thoughts about the themes of the novel and the construction of the text and image to realize these themes.

The second phase of ELLIE involved similar procedures except that in this phase we selected an electronic narrative or *e-book* for the children to read and respond to, and we used the ELLIE forums as a site for student discussion. Additionally, we involved some undergraduate students in working with small groups of children in Mark's class, to engage our students in classroom-based research related to children's literature and electronic literacies. The e-text we selected was one originally published by the BBC to accompany a television series, and was entitled *Spywatch*. The BBC have since taken the e-book off-line but educator Ben Clarke has (with permission) made it available for free download for teachers at: http://www.lookandread.fsnet.co.uk/downloads/ sites.html#spy. Additionally Ben Clarke's site (Clarke, 2000–2005) offers links to schools that have downloaded the software and then uploaded it to their own school servers, so the e-book is still active and accessible.

Spywatch is set in wartime England and traces the story of children who are investigating the townspeople to help the police discover a spy who is active in the town. The site makes good use of images, animations, sounds, hypertext and literacy challenges to unlock doors and solve clues to develop the narrative. It is multimodal, interactive, and combines games with the narrative to produce an exciting reading experience for younger children. Mark thought that although the story was targeted to children aged 7–9, it was at a suitable level for his older children for whom English was a second language. Similarly we thought it would also be suitable for the level of English required by the Finnish children.

Box 5.2 is an example of the staged series of lessons that Mark, the ELLIE research team and university students conducted with Mark's class. Teachers may like to take these lessons and adapt them to suit their own class and a buddy class or classes. The ELLIE website (Thomas, 2002–2005) is available for teachers to use for the lessons involving interaction between classes. More details about the ELLIE website are outlined in Chapter 6. Additional teaching notes are provided to assist teachers in conducting these lessons.

Box 5.2   Unit of work for non-English speaking background children

Learning about the construction of an e-book (*Spywatch*) and interacting with children from Finland to discuss and share understandings about the e-book.	
Lesson 1 Introduction to e-books; discussing the differences between printed books and e-books	• Ask children about their use of the internet and interactive on-line games. • Establish the special features they can identify such as animation and hyperlinks, and discuss purposes for these. • Explain to children that they will be reading an 'e-book' and ask them to predict what might be different in the e-book to printed books.
Lesson 2 Reading *Spywatch*	• In this session allow children to work in pairs to read and explore *Spywatch*. Children will need time to explore the site, to play some of the games, and to skip back and forth between narrative and game to uncover the clues and solve the puzzle of the e-book (i.e. who the spy in the town is).

Lesson 3
Focused reading:
examining the use of
images throughout
the text
	Teaching note: If computer lab time or internet time is limited, we suggest making a series of screenshots and printing out the hard copies to teach this lesson.
	• Children examine a series of images from *Spywatch* and respond to questions about the construction of the characters such as:
	  • Which characters in *Spywatch* are of high modality (see Chapter 1 for an explanation of modality)? Which are low? What effect does the modality have on your interaction with the different characters? Has the author done this on purpose? What effect is the author trying to create? (The author has purposefully varied the modality of the pictures to create a particular effect. For example, the author used higher modality pictures for the children helping us to solve the crime to help us feel more connected with them. The author used lower modality, cartoon-like pictures for the spies to distance the spies from us, making out the spies to be not like us and more easily seen as 'the villians'.)
	  • How do the characters look at us/engage us with offers or demands? At what times in the narrative are demands made? Do you notice any patterns in the use of offers and demands?

Lesson 4 Focused reading: examining the use of sound throughout the text	Provide children with the following challenges: • What sort of atmosphere does the music in *Spywatch* create? How does this suit the genre of the narrative? • Select an excerpt of *Spywatch* that has few sound effects or none at all and design some suitable accompanying music. Choose some instruments to use for your sound effects. Decide on the different ways to play the instrument to create different effects (such as tapping, blowing, thumping, playing certain notes, etc.). Write some music notation showing how you would use these different effects and other elements such as dynamics (loud and soft), and tempo (fast and slow) to create your sound effects.

	• Perform your sound effects while showing the relevant excerpts from *Spywatch* and explain the choices you made to create your notation.
Lesson 5 Focused reading: Examining the use of hypertext links throughout the narrative	• Make a list of the hyperlinks used in *Spywatch* and their role. (In *Spywatch*, hyperlinks are a unique feature of the e-text and provide extra information. They increase the interactivity of the story.) • Ask children to take an excerpt from a novel such as *Skellig* and suggest what words or phrases or images might be transformed into hyperlinks. Ask them to justify their selections in terms of the various purposes of hypertext, such as: to add further information; to explain a new concept; to show a close-up of a concept; to show a visual representation of a concept; to provide background information, and so on. Hyperlinks are sometimes thought of as a unique form of the textual conjunction (Morgan, 1999), so children could decide whether the word 'and', 'because' or 'for example' might be used to describe the hyperlinks.
Lesson 6 Focused reading: Examining the use of verbal grammar in the construction of the narrative	• Introduce the concept of modal adjuncts and modal verbs (see Chapter 1 for an introduction to modality). Provide children with examples of the same sentence but using varying degrees of modality, e.g: Suzanne: You **should** do your homework. Lillian: You **must** do your homework. Suzanne: Natasha is **always** good Lillian: Natasha is **usually** good. • Find an excerpt from a text which uses a range of modal operators (or write one to suit). Have students role-play it in small groups. Involve the children in a discussion about the effects of the different modals. • Read through the introduction of *Spywatch* and ask children to identify the modal words present (some of them are bolded and in capitals e.g., everyone **had to** go to a meeting, they **MUST** be spies). Ask children how the modal words add certain effects to the story, and ask them to

	exchange one modal word with another, stating how the meaning had been affected by using these types of modal operators (e.g. what does it make you think of the character? Does it change the way you think about the story? Does it change the mood being created? Why do you think the author used the modals they did rather than other ones?).
Lesson 7 Responding to text: writing first post on ELLIE	• Based on children's discussions and developing understandings about *Spywatch*, ask them to work in pairs to prepare a post which explains the most interesting things they have learned about *Spywatch* to share with the Finnish children. • Children post their responses to *Spywatch* on the ELLIE website. (Note: children had already used a forum to post their reviews and responses to the novel *Skellig*, so did not require a separate lesson learning how to post a message on-line. Children had also already spent time on general introductions, but this may take several interactions between the classes before proceeding to responses about the text.)
Lesson 8 Responding to text: writing posts to interact with Finnish children's ideas and add further ideas about the text.	• Children read each other's responses, and those of the Finnish children. Children are guided into a discussion on what they have learnt from the Finnish children and each other about *Spywatch*. Children are to write a follow-up post to respond to the Finnish children. • Teachers involved may like to extend their interactions with various focus questions on the text, depending upon children's needs. In our case, Mark and the Finnish teachers moved to work off-line (see lesson 9) and at a later date planned to share their e-text ideas with each other as a closure for the unit of interactive work.
Lesson 9 Transforming new understandings: creating a storyboard of own e-literature.	• Children list features of e-texts for use when developing their own e-text. • Examine other e-texts such as *Josie True* (www.josietrue.com) for elements of e-texts. Ask children prompt questions such as:

	• What are the textual features that make Spywatch and Josie True interesting, involving and informative? (students should be thinking of: pictures, hypertext, grammar, music, motion, games/ interaction) • What aspects of these features were manipulated to highlight the narrative features such as good and evil characters? (students should be thinking of: modality, offer/demand, genres, language use, etc.) • Students take a known story such as fairytale or a favourite novel and map out a hypertext, multimodal electronic version in storyboard form. The teacher may prompt with questions such as: • How can you make the narrative interactive? • How does the story progress? • How do the readers navigate from page to page or from section to section? • Where would it be appropriate to increase the images and decrease the text? • How can you make the text non-linear? • How have you engaged the reader through text/ pictures/hyperlinks? • How have you used music or sound effects to support the narrative? • Will there be only one possible ending, or several?
Lesson 10 Presenting storyboards.	• Children choose ways to share their storyboards. Depending upon time and resources, the children may do one or more of the following: • Take digital images to include in their e-text. • Draw, paint or create digital art images for the e-text. • Compose and notate music and sound effects to include in their e-text. • Map out a layout for an on-line version of the e-text. • Create a PowerPoint version of the e-text to feature the hyperlinked narrative.

	• Storyboards may be displayed around the classroom, or compiled into a class ideas book. Ideally they could be published on-line for children in Finland (or other buddy classes) to enjoy.

Snapshot 3: Coco

Coco is a teacher in Quebec, Canada. She teaches elementary children aged 10–12. Coco is very active in on-line communities related to both teaching and her own personal hobbies. She is on several mailing lists related to using technology in the classroom, and regularly engages in on-line discussions with colleagues. In 1999, Coco first began thinking about how to take her class to the on-line visual worlds of the palace. To begin with, the purpose she had in mind was to encourage children to practise their English with native speakers. As Coco explored the possibilities of the palace, she ventured into the palace *Kids, Enfants, Kinder* (Thomas, 1999–2003) and observed children engaged in interactive role-playing and storying (see Chapter 4 for a discussion of one example of this). Coco decided to use the literature and narrative writing focus of this palace with her children.

In the first instance, Coco organized children into small groups to use the room backgrounds as a stimulus for interactive storybuilding. Storybuilding is a technique where the teacher carefully guides children's responses to questions about a stimulus to structure a narrative. The questions are used as a framing device to ensure that the narrative is structured according to the generic schematic structure of a narrative, i.e. it begins with an orientation that introduces the characters, settings and circumstances of the story, it has a series of events which lead progressively more to a complication and climax, and concludes with a resolution of that complication. Questions are carefully thought out by the teacher prior to the lesson. As children take turns responding to the questions, the narrative develops and takes shape. The teacher may need to probe with unplanned questions to deepen the responses given by children.

As the narrative develops through the storybuilding activity, children are told they need to be accepting of the responses by others (sometimes the teacher may need to intervene if a child gives an inappropriate response that doesn't fit with the established narrative). However, often children indicate that they were thinking of other ideas to the ones offered by their classmates, and that the storybuilding has stimulated their creative thinking. To this end, it is often good practice to finish the storybuilding by inviting children (individually or in pairs) to write their own version of the narrative, which may use any, all or only some of the responses developed collaboratively.

Stimuli for interactive storybuilding can include interesting images, old objects (such as an old children's shoe), a page ostensibly torn from an old diary (e.g. the teacher may write an imaginary diary entry on a piece of paper, and burn the edges or drag a teabag over it to make it look old and mysterious), a recording of a voice in distress, a postcard with some mysterious text on the back of it, an old photo, and so on. Coco's children were familiar with this concept and had engaged in a number of interactive storybuilding activities in their literacy programmes throughout the year. Unsure of how to introduce her children to the on-line role-playing, Coco thought that using the background images in the palace as a stimulus for storybuilding would provide sufficiently familiar structure to the children to introduce them to the virtual environment without it becoming threatening to any of them. Figure 5.2 shows a small group of Coco's children in the palace.

Using this room background, children responded to a series of questions to develop the narrative. Box 5.3 is an example of a framework used by Coco in

Figure 5.2   Coco's children engaged in interactive storybuilding on the palace

Box 5.3   Storybuilding using the room background at the palace as a stimulus

Framework of questions

1. Somebody lives alone in the castle on the hill. That person has not left the castle grounds for over ten years. Is the person a male or a female?
2. How old is s/he?
3. What is his/her first name?
4. What colour/length/type is his/her hair?
5. There is something interesting about this person's (insert the children's selected name for the person from here on) hands, tell us what it is.
6. There is one distinguishing, striking feature about the person, what is it?
7. The person doesn't have a happy demeanour – describe the expression that is usually seen on the person's face.
8. Did s/he always live alone there?
9. The castle is very large for one person – describe the person's favourite room.
10. Why is this room their favourite room?
11. In the room is a photo of this person when she/he was a child. He/she looks very like they are laughing. Who took this photo?
12. Where is the person when this photo was taken?
13. What happened to cause the laughter seen in the photo?
14. Looking about in the room, there is another item that seems like a special keep-sake for the person. What is it?
15. Describe this thing.
16. What makes it so special to the person?
17. The castle is so isolated up on that hill. How does the person get supplies such as food?
18. Is the person healthy?
19. Does he/she do any exercise?
20. Describe a typical day for this person (this question could be divided up into morning, afternoon and night to make three questions).
21. Late one afternoon, the person goes into their favourite room. Describe his/her movements in the room.
22. The person seems to be particularly distressed this particular afternoon, what is the news that has caused this?
23. The person has decided to write a letter. Who is he/she writing it to?
24. What does he/she write in the letter?
25. Why is it so important for the person to send this letter immediately?
26. For some reason, the letter can't be sent in the usual way, what is this reason?
27. How does the person decide to overcome this dilemma?
28. Describe the events that followed this decision.
29. By the end of this day, the expression on the person's face has changed. Describe this changed expression.
30. One year later, the person is no longer living in the castle alone. Who or what is living there with them?

this storybuilding exercise. The framework begins with some simple and basic questions, but as the narrative is developed, the questions are more probing. The simple questions at the beginning are necessary for creating a shared understanding of the details from which more creative ideas can flow. The framework is devised to focus on one small aspect of a narrative and as such it also provokes further questions without offering children the opportunity to answer them in this specific session. This leaves space for later creative and imaginative writing.

The storybuilding activity was a safe, risk-free experience to offer the children, and it was one that didn't involve children from other countries. What it did do was to encourage confidence in Coco, the children, and the children's parents about the environment of the palace. Coco reported that children were not only creatively stimulated from this experience on the palace, but they were highly enthusiastic and excited and constantly asking for more – so much so that she decided to introduce them to the interactive on-line role-playing of the palace related to the Greek myth of Demeter and Persephone. Coco's class was one of the classes reported upon in Chapter 4. The interactive role-playing was conducted in English and with children from other countries, so Coco's initial purpose of engaging children in speaking English with native speakers was achieved. It was achieved, however, with much more breadth and depth in terms of curriculum outcomes than she had ever first imagined was possible.

Conclusion

In this chapter we have presented snapshots of the classroom work undertaken by three teachers: Jenny, Mark and Coco, in their quests to integrate information and communication technologies into their work with children's literature and literacy. Each of these teachers has generously offered detailed examples of classroom planning to provide ideas that cater for a wide range of children. These have included classes of younger children, children in English-speaking countries who speak English as a second language, children from non-English-speaking countries, and classes of older children. The lessons also showcase a variety of uses of ICT, such as using websites, exploring e-books, using discussion forums, and using the virtual world of the palace. Teachers are becoming increasingly more creative in their integration of ICT into the curriculum, and are using and exploiting the affordances of ICT to maximum potential. The teachers whose classroom work is discussed in this chapter are just such teachers.

6 Middle Earth meets the Matrix!
Teachers researching classroom practice using ICT and children's literature

Introduction

In previous chapters we have presented a range of transformative classroom literacy practices involving the use of children's literature and the affordances of information and communication technologies. These classroom practices have included: reading and working with CD-ROMs and literature-based websites (Chapter 2); talking about children's literature in on-line contexts such as book raps (Chapter 3); reading, writing and performing in character the literary narratives of a role-playing MUD or palace (Chapter 4); and discussing e-books in electronic forums (Chapter 5). In summary, the classroom experiences presented have required children to engage in the reading, writing and creating of a range of multi-modal texts for varying purposes, showcasing a diverse range of literacies throughout the book. In presenting new ways of using children's literature, we have also emphasized the value and richness of existing classroom practices, and have offered these new ways as opportunities to enhance and develop classroom literacy programs.

In this chapter, we offer a challenge for teachers to undertake a programme of work that adopts the new transformative literacy practices. We invite teachers to trial an action research project with the intention of exploring the potential for using digital technologies in the literacy classroom in the ways we have discussed in this book. We outline a research plan that starts with explaining how to initiate a study, and we provide the tools to begin the research. We offer a series of lesson ideas, teaching strategies and methods of observing and analyzing what children are doing with children's literature and ICT in this programme. We also offer a means of communicating the research outcomes, through publication on the ELLIE (Electronic Literature and Literacies in International Education) website. Our aim is to collect teachers' reports about the research to share with others, and to develop a network of educators who are willing to trial and explore the most effective means of developing children's literacy skills in digital contexts.

Teachers and students as co-researchers – implementing transformative literacy practices

In explaining action research, Mills states that it is a systematic inquiry by educators to gather information about practices of teaching and student learning 'with the goals of gaining insight, developing reflective practice, effecting positive changes in the school environment and the lives of those involved' (2003: 5). We would like to adopt the four key concepts of action research as defined by Mills to frame up the research project we are presenting here. We will now discuss each of these concepts in turn.

Key concept one is that the research is 'participatory and democratic'. We hope teachers reading this book will have felt challenged and inspired to explore some new ways of including ICT into everyday practices with children's literature. We hope many of our readers will trial some of the ideas we have presented. But we also want teachers to take a critical stance in doing this, by investigating the value and impact of adopting the ideas we suggest. In the project presented here, we invite feedback and offer an opportunity for teachers (and children) to post reports and observations on a public forum (the ELLIE forum, described in more detail later). We want to know if your use of ICT in your programmes has made a positive difference.

Key concept two is that action research is 'socially responsive and takes place in context'. In our experiences, we have talked with many teachers who are aware that the internet is fast impacting on many aspects of life, and who believe that it is important to respond to the changes in society by using the internet in their classrooms. Cope and Kalantzis (1999) have challenged teachers for some years now to prepare children for 'successful social futures' by providing them with the literacy skills they need for living in the Information Age. Knobel (1999) has presented a number of case studies in which children are finding vast incongruities between their literacy practices outside of school involving technology, and the traditional literacy practices inside their classroom walls. It is becoming more frequent now in classrooms to have children with more knowledge and experience in a particular context than their teachers. We believe it is a perfect time for teachers to learn more about the uses of ICT in meaningful ways in the classroom to enhance and support existing practices, and to take into account the everyday literacy practices in which many of the students of the Information Age are already involved.

Key concept three is that action research 'helps teacher researchers examine the everyday, taken-for-granted ways in which they carry out professional practice'. We are very interested in the existing practices of teachers when working with literary texts in the classroom. It is important for us to determine how teachers can effectively integrate ICT into the professional work they do as a matter of course. We are also interested in English teachers sharing best practices in an international context, developing networks and discovering together what works best and how to do it. Our hope is that through sharing experiences, we can learn from each other. The research design to be presented below will be a starting point for what we hope to be a productive experience for all participants in understanding and developing transformative literacy practices.

Finally, key concept four is that 'knowledge gained through action research can liberate students, teachers, and administrators and enhance learning, teaching, and policy-making'. We encourage all of our readers who embrace this research project to share what they have learned through it with others – with colleague teachers, the school community, parent groups, and the community at large. Our intention with this book is to offer a guide for teachers to explore new ideas in a supportive context. We expect that students involved will not only find participating on-line an exciting and fun experience, but that the experience will be one which challenges, demands, and takes their literacy skills to new levels. We also envisage that students with experience in on-line contexts will be empowered to become co-constructors of their own learning, by contributing ideas and working more collaboratively with the teacher throughout the programme. Liberating indeed! We hope that this 'on the ground' research work will provide new avenues for other teachers in the future, and that in fact the experiences of our readers will impact at the policy level in the future.

These key concepts of action research encapsulate the excitement and enthusiasm we have in inviting our readers to become involved with us in a common research project, to share our reports, and to discover together new ways of using ICT in the English classroom. We see our role as an enabling one – enabling teachers to generate clear and critical ways forward to improve and enhance children's learning. Through engaging in this project and participating in a global community, we believe that together we can make a difference to the quality of children's literacy learning in classrooms.

The classroom research project: Middle Earth Meets the Matrix!

This research project will centre on a study of the world of Tolkien: Middle Earth. We will present a series of lesson ideas as we articulate the research design. It is important to keep a clear research focus in mind throughout the programme, and this begins with defining our research question(s). We suggest the following:

- In what ways (if any) is children's literacy enhanced through their participation on-line?

- What (if anything) did the children learn through their on-line participation that they could not have achieved off-line?

Teachers may also have questions in mind such as 'How does this enhance my existing practice?' These questions should help focus and inform the ways of observing what happens throughout the project. The answers to these questions will be determined through collecting information at various stages of the project.

In Chapter 4 we introduced the on-line visual worlds of palaces, sites for interactive communication and role-playing. The main site for the research will be at the Middle Earth palace (Sorenson, 2000–2005, on-line), a g-rated visual virtual world. Instructions and free software required for joining this site are outlined in detail at the Middle Earth palace website (RAGTime, 2002). The palace is owned by Laurie Sorenson, or, as she prefers to be called on-line, 'Nimue', and she and her volunteer staff are all Tolkien aficionados. The community members (ranging from age 11 to 70), have names such as 'Elrond' and 'Hobbitness' and they come from many different countries, including England, the USA, Holland, and Australia. The palace is replete with beautiful art work traversing all of Tolkien's magical lands, from the Shire to Lothlorien to Helm's Deep. Many rooms have sound bytes from the movie versions of the books, and each room has a drop-down help menu for beginners, covering basics like movement from room to room in the palace, and a map showing where you are located in Middle Earth. Avatars of hobbits, elves and the other citizens of Middle Earth are hidden away in rooms like Easter eggs, and children will find great enjoyment hunting and collecting them. Some of the Middle Earth community members like to speak Elvish (but always offer translations for the novice), others like to dance and sing songs or recite poetry in the Hobbit tradition. Middle Earth also has an associated website and web forum, as well as a text-based fantasy role-playing site.

The Middle Earth website provides information about the palace, including a list of staff members, the rules for participating, general background information, instructions for joining, and sample rooms to show what the palace environment is like, such as Figure 6.1.

The website describes the palace environment as follows:

> Middle Earth is an interactive graphical chat environment, built by and for Tolkien fans! For those of you who think 'chat' on the internet is only 'text on a screen', you are in for a pleasant surprise . . . oh yes precious . . . pleasant suprisssess . . . Middle Earth is made up of interconnecting chat rooms that are animated and scripted. You can navigate with maps or take one of our tours of the books or the movies. Our guests can interact with the rooms and other guests by moving

Figure 6.1 Sample palace room at Middle Earth

around on the screen, chatting, activating scripts and by wearing avatars.

(RAGTime, 2002, on-line)

We have selected this particular palace as the research site for a number of reasons:

- It is an excellent example of a role-playing palace of the nature described in Chapter 4.
- It is g-rated and this is strictly enforced by the staff, so children can be ensured of a safe on-line learning environment.
- The worlds and words of Tolkien are enchanting to many age

groups, and provide a rich literary focus in which children can be immersed.

- The palace has a number of in-built tutorials for beginners.
- The staff (the Gods and wizards) and community members are friendly, fun, and more than willing to support teachers in their work. The owner is very enthusiastic about the prospect of teachers and their classes of students visiting and is happy to make any modifications or to add features to the palace if asked.
- There is an 'Instant Palace' version of Middle Earth, which means that it can be accessed directly through a web browser.
- The palace has many existing fun features, such as the hidden avatars, the music, the animated room images, maps, information, links to Tolkien websites, and a dedicated website and newsgroup for discussion.

Sharing the research outcomes (ELLIE)

We have created a research website with a focus on investigating 'Electronic Literature and Literacies in International Education': the ELLIE website (Thomas, 2002–2005). On this website we have started publishing ideas and examples of research projects. The site has an in-built discussion forum that was discussed in Chapter 5. On the website we have also started compiling a range of web-based resources which may support teachers in undertaking the 'Middle Earth Meets the Matrix' research project. Below we have identified a number of stages throughout the project when teachers might submit material to the website. We invite teachers to engage in forum discussions and in the submission of observations, impressions, and children's sample creations at all stages of the project. This will provide a valuable support network for all participants in the project, with opportunities to manage any difficulties experienced, and to seek assistance in understanding and interpreting the data collected. As more participants share their reports, we will work together to answer the research questions.

Managing the project

Box 6.1 is the outline of suggested lessons matched with various stages of the research design. This project is suitable for children aged approximately 10–14 years of age. The lessons are designed to give children time to immerse themselves in the rich world of Tolkien through both on-line and off-line experiences. The end point of the lessons is an on-line role-play on the Middle Earth palace. The lessons are meant as a guide only, and we expect that the

Box 6.1   The Middle Earth Meets the Matrix Research Project

Potential curriculum outcomes

Through this unit of work it is anticipated that students will do the following:
- Revise the grammatical features of narratives and use these to co-construct their own narratives.
- Discuss in detail the genre of fantasy and in particular, the Hero's quest, through comparing examples of literature across different cultures reflecting this genre, and through writing in this genre.
- Conduct detailed investigations of the type of language used by different Middle Earth characters in varying contexts (i.e. type of vocabulary used by different characters, the language of songs and poems used by the Hobbits, an investigation into the Elvish language, a study of riddles as used by Bilbo Baggins in the cave, as well as the rich language of fantasy and description used by Tolkien).
- Be able to describe and critique the style of Tolkien's writing.
- Write, illustrate and participate in an extended fantasy story, drawing upon knowledge of the genre.
- Practise and use sophisticated, extended vocabulary as appropriate to characters and the fantasy context.
- Use technology to create texts and images (e.g. avatars).
- Demonstrate a high degree of technological literacy through effectively participating in literary events in the digital context.

Lesson focus	Lesson details	Research focus
1. Reading *The Hobbit*	Teacher reading class novel: *The Hobbit*	These first lessons are setting the stage for the research. They are designed to immerse the children in the worlds and words of Tolkien, to create enthusiasm and to provoke curiosity.
	Teachers may also like to show the film version of the *The Hobbit*, and compare the film and book versions.	
	During reading, the teacher may invite some guided discussions about the characters and Bilbo's journey, such as *What hints does the narrator give that the cave will not be the safe shelter the dwarves hope for?* in Chapter 4.	
	There are numerous teacher guides to assist children in reading and understanding the text. Some on-line resources such as the Teachers @	

	Random House website (Random House, 2004, on-line) and the Webster School District website (2004, on-line) provide valuable examples if teachers are looking for ideas. Teachers may like to seek out an appropriate book rap as described in Chapter 3 to talk with other classes about *The Hobbit*.	
2. Creating a story map	Children design a map of Bilbo Baggins' journey through Middle Earth. Children can use Tolkien's rich descriptive language as a source for guiding their illustrations.	Teacher begins recording observations of the language use of children with focus questions such as: • Are the children using any specialized language to describe the journey? • How do children talk about their choices of images used to illustrate the map?
3. Character studies	Children research characters in mythology such as elves, hobbits, dwarves etc. They may: • write descriptions (using knowledge of features of descriptions, such as detailed noun groups using a range of adjective types), • draw images (using knowledge of visual grammar as a guide), • discuss qualities of characters such as bravery Using ideas by Lawrence (1987), we suggest further exploration of the	Teacher continues to record observations of children's use of language and image. Teacher also compiles a list of resources and associated websites that best assist children in their developing understandings – a list of resources used by teachers will be published at the ELLIE

	characters through games such as 'name the character', which involves allocating the students a character to research, and then to write clues, draw pictures and/or role-play the character in front of the group who have to guess which character it is.	website so teachers are invited to contribute their ideas to this resource list.
4. Introduction to the Middle Earth palace	Teachers take the children onto the palace and give them time to explore its features. A quick way of exploring is directly through the web using the 'Instant Palace' version: (http://middleearthpalace.com:9984/palace/client/instantpal.html). However, not all of the features are available through instant palace, so we recommend teachers download the free software 'palace client' and connect using that. As previously mentioned, this software can be downloaded from the Middle Earth palace website. We also recommend that teachers visit the palace a number of times prior to the children to familiarize themselves with the features of the site, the rules, the staff, and so on. This exploration phase of the project may take some weeks, as the learning curve may be quite steep. We suggest doing the beginner tutorials to best understand the technicalities of the space.	During this phase we suggest the teacher keep a journal of reflections and observations about the experiences had both by themselves when first visiting the palace, and by the children as they explore. It would be valuable to tape record pairs of children at a time to examine the language they used as they explored, negotiated and discovered the world of the Middle Earth palace.
5. Creating a character for role-play	In this series of lessons we recommend that teachers use the Maricopa website (MCLI, 2000, on-line) guide to creating characters for 'a hero's story' in preparation for their role-playing in part 7 of the project. This site provides a scaffold	Character descriptions and photo albums should be collected as artefacts for sharing and for future examination.

	for children to develop an original and rich background for their characters, rather than relying on using the popular characters from Tolkien's book.	
	This scaffold asks children to consider where their character was born, what their favourite pastimes when growing up were, what their special talents were and so on. This background information will provide a strong foundation for the in-role action to come.	
	Once children have developed their character, another way to consolidate the background information would be to ask children to create a small photo album of their character's life. Children could also write captions to support their 'photos'.	
6. Creating character texts and images.	Teacher selects various sections of the Hobbit to highlight some of the specialized language use by Tolkien and by particular characters (for example, the rich language used by Tolkien to describe both characters and places; the songs of the dwarves (Chapter 1), or the goblins (Chapter 4); the Elvish language (examples might also be taken from *Lord of the Rings*); and the riddles used by Bilbo and Gollum (Chapter 5).	Texts and images created by the children should be collected for sharing on the ELLIE website and also for analysis.
	Children create texts and images for role-play: songs, riddles, greetings in Elvish, character expressions, selection of avatars and props.	
	A detailed list of web-based resources to assist teachers and children in this process (for example, tutorials in elvish, tutorials in making avatars) are listed on the ELLIE website.	

7. Role-playing on the palace: the palace quest.	Everything has been leading up to the role-playing.	Transcripts of the role-play should be kept for analysis.
	The structure of the 'hero's quest' genre is outlined in a number of on-line resources (e.g. the Random House website identified in session one above). The teacher should discuss the structure and engage children in identifying the elements in both *The Hobbit* and other examples of quest texts.	If teachers have video facilities, a video of the role-playing would be valuable to capture the visual elements of the experience.
	The role-playing should follow the three key steps of a quest: the departure, the initiation and the return. During each of these stages the teacher should organize for a particular child or a parent helper (or one of the Middle Earth community members) to go in role as a guide to move the narrative successfully through each stage.	After some time has been spent conducting preliminary analyses, we invite teachers to share reports of their project on-line at the ELLIE website.
	Role-playing is best done in small groups of probably no more than 8–10 children. Groups could be identified from session five above so that children could work together to select characters that could be involved in the quest together. Children could be involved in making decisions about the narrative out of role throughout the stages of the role-playing.	Teachers may like to use the forums on ELLIE to seek support in analyzing the role-playing transcripts together, or in discussing any issues or ideas that arose during this (or any) stage of the research process.
	Details of a possible quest to take and the structures and stages of the quest are detailed below.	
	At the conclusion of the quest, the teacher may like to extend the unit of work and have children write scripts based on their role-play. Children may like to recreate the on-line scenes off-line, or they may like to repeat the	

	quest with their scripted lines. Teachers are invited to share any additional ideas on the ELLIE website.	

program will be adapted in numerous ways to suit the particular needs of the class of children, and also to best meet the curriculum demands of each teacher's respective school, education department and country. In the project design below we have also identified how the suggested lessons may in fact meet such curriculum demands.

The role-play in Middle Earth: the quest to save Mithradir

The following role-play in Box 6.2 has been designed with the kind assistance of the members of the Middle Earth community. It is important for the teacher to first email the owner, Nimue, to discuss times and organize the groups so that community assistance is available during the role-play. The teacher should also email the project manager, Angela Thomas (a.thomas@edfac. usyd.edu.au), to enable access to ELLIE forums and be directed to resources necessary. Contact details are included at the end of this chapter. We suggest the teacher work through the role-play rooms first without the children to become familiar with how it works.

A further note about meeting curriculum demands

It is anticipated that the stages in the programme of work (fun!) will be suited to varying modes of organization by the teacher. The reading of *The Hobbit* and study of Elvish will clearly be a whole-class shared activity. Creating characters would best be independent group tasks, while any stage where children are actually on-line in Middle Earth should be a strictly supervised and guided group task. We have suggested that on-line role-playing best be organized in groups of no more than eight to ten children. However, the number of computers with on-line access and the location of these computers may impact upon group size. Ideally, a minimum of four on-line computers would be required to best engage children in all experiences in the programme of work. It would be valuable to invite parents to be part of the on-line experiences too – not just for practical purposes of assisting teachers, but also to create a wider excitement and enthusiasm for the project. It would also offer parents an opportunity to learn something new about the technological world that they might not otherwise have a chance to do. In this way, children will also realize that learning is a lifelong process.

Box 6.2 Details of the role-play

The role-play will take approximately three 1 hour sessions. It is designed to be both challenging and fun. At various stages a group of children may need to do further work off-line to progress their quest. The role-playing uses techniques of experiential drama such as 'teacher-in-role', 'still images', 'storytelling', 'image making', and 'writing in role' (Neelands and Goode, 2000; O'Neill, 1995; Taylor, 2000). It also makes use of the affordances of the palace, such as animated scripting, on-line virtual theatre, avatar creation, and specialized coding commands. Children are required to use both language and image for a range of purposes within the overall quest.

Palace room	Drama stage and strategy	Details of stage
Hobbiton Smials Mallorn Glade	1. Group improvised role-play to familiarize each other with characters and to begin the process of enrolling.	Children meet at *Hobbiton Smials* and are told that all of their characters have been called to a Middle Earth assembly to hear some important news. The assembly is held in the room on the palace called *Mallorn Glade*, which is in the Woods of Lothlorien. There will be a picnic feast waiting for them upon their arrival to the meeting place so the characters can meet each other, introduce each other and talk together (in role) over food as they wonder what the important news will be.
Mallorn Glade	2. Teacher in role to establish the purpose of quest and guide the action.	The teacher comes on in role as the blue wizard Pallando. Children are told by Pallando that a young elf named Mithradir was playing with his friend, Curunir in the valley of Rivendell, when the evil dragon Scatha swooped down and snatched Mithradir in his talons, flying away. Pallando says that he is unable to use his wizardly powers in Middle Earth, but will help direct them to Elrond, since only Elrond, leader of the elves, has the special gift of foresight. Only Elrond may be able to reveal whether or not Mithradir is alive, and if so, where he is being held. Pallando directs the children to the entrance of Lothlorien, the *Elven Escort* room.

Elven Escort Advice of the Lady The Silverlode Two Rivers Meet Haldir's Picnic	3. Teacher in role to respond to children's questions, to encourage speaking phrases in Elvish, and to further the quest.	Children are to go to the room *Elven Escort* to take the swan boat ride (click the start button to commence the boat ride, to be taken two people at a time) along the rivers Nimrodel and Silverlode to Lothlorien. When they arrive, the teacher (or a parent, or one of the children) can go in role as Elrond to be questioned by the children about the whereabouts of Mithradir. When the children arrive, they are surprised to realize that Elrond only speaks Elvish, so they may need to go and seek translation assistance from the web or from one of the community members of Middle Earth to seek Elrond's assistance. Elrond tells the children: 'At the bottom of the falls of Henneth Annun in Ithilien sits Gollum, and only Gollum has seen the path taken by the dragon.' Elrond also gives the characters a fish (an avatar of the fish is hidden in the room *Haldir's Picnic*, and can be retrieved by clicking on the image of the bird) and tells them that they may need the fish to summon Gollum.
The Forbidden Pool The Oliphant The Forbidden Pool Ruins in Ithilien	4. Teacher in role, children questioning, telling riddles, following clues.	Children are to hunt for the room that meets this description (the room is actually called *The Forbidden Pool* in the lands of Gondor and Gollum appears after a click at the bottom of the pool OR if the children are wearing the fish avatar, but children should be given time to explore the clues given by Elrond to try to find the room themselves). The teacher (or a parent, or one of the children, or a Middle Earth community member) is to go in role as Gollum and demand that the characters entertain him with riddles before he gives away any clues as to Mithradir's whereabouts. After the children have told a few riddles, Gollum tells them the next clue: 'Grey as mouse,

		big as a house, nose like a snake, I make the earth shake. As I tramp through the grass, trees crack as I pass, with horns in my mouth I walk in the South. Flapping big ears, beyond count of years, I stump round and round, never lie on the ground . . .' Find me, then click the glowing horse twice, then ask the old man of the ruins for your next clue (click on his head but be sure you are holding the ancient rune as you do so).
Ruins in Ithilien	5. Clue-seeking	The ancient man of the runes speaks: 'Scatha has hidden the elf you speak of in his treasure cave. There is a secret password you need to type to take you directly to speak to Scatha. Shall I tell you? You must beware though, as Scatha will need a great deal of convincing to give you custody of Mithradir! The secret code you must type in exactly is: "Yala onna" (Yala onna is elvish for "summon creature", and as each child says this phrase, they are transported into the room called *The Hoard*). It is an image of a dragon with a hoard of treasures'.
The Hoard	6. Teacher-in-role to provoke children's use of persuasive language, problem solving and further research about aspects of mythology.	The teacher or assigned person is to go in role as the dragon, Scatha. The teacher should hiss and spit and crackle and flame appropriately during this role-playing session. The teacher (dragon) should at first absolutely refuse to return Mithradir, and tell the children that they must have a convincing argument to persuade her. At this stage the children might want to go out of role and discuss what they know about dragons in mythology, and problem solve what might work to charm or convince the dragon to return Mithradir. They may need to revise their understandings of the genre of argument and persuasive language, they may decide to make small

		avatar props of gifts for the dragon, or they may decide to create song lyrics to charm it. Children may also like to re-read Chapter 12 of *The Hobbit*, which has descriptions of the dragon Smaug. The teacher could point out the flattering language that Bilbo uses to speak to Smaug, such as 'O Smaug the Tremendous' and 'O Smaug the Chiefest and Greatest of Calamities' (Tolkien, 1937). They are then to return to the room to try to charm the dragon. The teacher is to continue being difficult to persuade to really make the children extend their use of language at this stage. Finally, when the teacher feels the children have worked hard enough (!), the dragon can tell them that the only way he will return Mithradir is if the children retrieve its treasured Arkenstone which was taken by the dwarves some years previously. The Arkenstone is the one ancient jewel coveted most by the greedy dragon! The children will have to ask how to find it, and the dragon can tell them that there is a secret entrance to the dwarves' treasures in Moria somewhere, marked by the symbol of an ancient rune.
Moria Hall Dwarf Lobby Various rooms of Isengard The Hoard	7. Improvised role-play, treasure hunt, resolving the problem, completing the quest and returning home.	Children search for the clues until they find the room called *Moria Hall*, at which they speak the secret password (Moria) to enter the room with the hoard of treasure. A group of dwarves are guarding the treasure in the room and demand to know what the children are doing there. The children then need to ask for the Arkenstone. The dwarves make the children explain why they want it, then offer them the Arkenstone only if they can return with the seven golden artefacts of Isengard. The golden artefacts are props hidden in various rooms of

		Isengard, and can be obtained by spotting and clicking on the secret rune symbol. Upon collection, the children return to the dwarves and offer up the seven artefacts (dropping the seven props). Once all seven props are dropped, they will each be given a piece of the Arkenstone, which they have to cooperate to piece together like a jigsaw, then they can return to the room called *The Hoard* to give the Arkenstone to the dragon, Scatha. Once the Arkenstone is dropped in the dragon's lair, the missing elf, Mithradir, will appear, and they will all be transported back to the *Mallorn Glade*.
Mallorn Glade	8. Storytelling in role	Upon their return, the children can tell the stories of the quest to the concerned family and friends in Lothlorien. It would be fun if the school principal or the children's parents were on-line waiting for the questing characters to listen to the stories. One of the children might like to go in role as Mithradir to tell how frightened it was in Scatha's cave and how grateful he was to the rescuers. The teacher might like to add in a curious ending by commenting that Mithradir's friend Curunir who was with him at the time of the kidnapping by the dragon 'looked none too pleased to see his friend again, though masked his displeasure by a thin smile'. This might pave the way for further writing in role, or further role-playing in the future.
Mallorn Glade	9. Reflection on the role-play through writing, drawing, retelling and discussing what was learned.	The teacher should spend some time off-line with the children to allow them to tell their stories again, both in role, and then out of role. Groups might like to retell their quest in a series of still photos, or in song, or through writing, to share with others.

Collecting the research data

Above we have outlined times throughout the project during which observations of various activities may be collected. In addition to observations, we have recommended other types of data also be collected. These included: collecting artefacts such as the text and images created by students as preparation for their virtual role-playing; keeping transcripts of the palace logs of the role-playing and using the video and associated storyboards to examine language use. Methods of analysis are discussed below. Additionally, we suggest giving the children a questionnaire asking them to describe what they learned throughout the unit. The questionnaire could ask such questions as:

- What did you enjoy most about the work you did on Middle Earth?
- What three things did you learn that were completely new to you?
- What else would you have liked to do about Middle Earth that you didn't get time to do?
- Did your teacher or your parents think you did something special in this unit of work that you hadn't done before?

As Mills states, '[I]t is generally accepted in action research circles that researchers should not rely on any single source of data, interview, observation, or instrument' (2003: 52). Using a range of sources is termed 'triangulation' and it is recommended to ensure that varying perspectives can be closely examined to understand complex phenomena. It also provides a systematic and rigorous way to ensure that the conclusions from the research are clear and well supported. The matrix in Table 6.1 reflects the research design taking into account the need for triangulation.

Analyzing the research data

As Stake asserts, 'there is no particular moment when data analysis begins . . . [a]nalysis essentially means taking something apart. We take our impressions, our observations apart' (1995: 71). It is for this reason that we have emphasized the posting of observations and data on the ELLIE website at many stages throughout the research project. By sharing observations with other teachers, we expect that discussions will ensue that will assist in the interpretation of those observations. The questionnaires given to children will also elicit from them the degree of learning they believe they have achieved through the programme, and what they say about their own learning will provide an excellent avenue for discussion and analysis. Some teachers may feel that reflecting upon their observations and the children's comments will provide them with the answers to the research questions. However, in addition to the observations and questionnaires, there is one other specific research tool

Table 6.1 Research data collection

	Data source		
Research questions	1	2	3
In what ways (if any) are children's literacy skills enhanced through their participation on-line?	Observations and field notes recorded by teacher	Artefacts created by children for on-line participation: avatars, songs, elvish texts	Role-playing logs – transcripts of interactions
What (if anything) did the children learn through their on-line participation that they could not have achieved off-line?	Teacher records of children's literacy achievements prior to the research project	Artefacts children have created in previous units of off-line work for comparison	Questionnaires given to children

we wish to suggest teachers use together to understand and interpret the data collected. This is a discourse analysis (both text and image) of the artefacts and role-playing logs created by children.

Discourse analysis provides a means for looking closely at the ways in which children have used language and images to construct their texts. Our first research question, 'In what ways (if any) are children's literacy skills enhanced through their participation on-line?' requires an inspection of the level of literacy demonstrated in the texts constructed by the children. The second question, 'What (if anything) did the children learn through their on-line participation that they could not have achieved off-line?' requires a close inspection of the role-playing logs and a comparison between this and other texts created by children. We would like to propose a basic ten-step process to the discourse analysis:

1 Looking back over your observations, what are the common themes or patterns you can identify that seem significant?
2 Reading through the artefacts children made, what grammatical features of narrative (or other genres where appropriate) are evidenced, and what in particular stands out as remarkable or unexpected?
3 Viewing the images children created in the various artefacts, what visual grammar features are evidenced, and does anything stand out as remarkable or unexpected?
4 What intertextuality is evidenced through the children's role-playing

(i.e. what are the other texts that children draw from in order to successfully participate in the role-play)?

5   In responding to the questionnaire, what are the common themes children mentioned that seem significant?

6   In what ways did you observe children adopting or exercising power throughout both the on-line and off-line experiences?

7   In what ways did individual children construct a sense of the character they were role-playing, and what elements of the real child did you see reflected in the character?

8   When discussing their experiences, what statements did children make when referring to themselves, i.e. what 'I-statements' (Gee, 1999: 124) did they make?

9   What words or phrases used by children seemed particularly important in the role-playing context?

10   Overall, what did children learn about *The Hobbit* in this unit that seemed unique or different to what they have learned in other units on similar children's literature, and to what would you attribute this?

This is a starting point for the analysis. For teachers wanting to learn more about techniques of textual and visual discourse analysis, we recommend the following references: Phillips and Jorgensen (2002), Gee (1999), Kress and van Leeuwen (2001), and Rose (2001). As a conclusion to the analysis we invite teachers to write a report of their experiences, reflections and findings from the research project. We will collate these reports and publish them at the ELLIE website, and (ideally) into a future print publication.

Further research possibilities

The 'Middle Earth Meets the Matrix' research project is one exemplar of the type of research project that could be undertaken by teachers to investigate meaningful ways of incorporating ICT and children's literature in classroom practice. However, there are other palaces and on-line forums dedicated to children's literature that could also work as a viable starting point for a similar type of research project. The palaces *Hogwarts* (Maykitten, 2004), *Harry Potters* (Aurora, 2004), and *Bloody Brilliant* (Layke, 2004), are dedicated to Harry Potter fans and have related websites/discussion forums. The palace *Nexus Quest* (Souza, 2004) and related website is dedicated to Pokémon fans. There are a number of anime palaces dedicated to Japanese fantasy quests. Some palaces have themes based on Arthurian legend or Greek mythology. A directory of all palaces and a description of the palaces is book marked in the palace software, so teachers can explore the range of sites and select one that best suits the needs of the class. A word of caution, however, we have not talked with staff members of each palace and cannot recommend that any palace apart from Middle Earth will be suitable for a research project with children. Teachers should explore the palace site thoroughly and seek permission from its owners to ensure that children will be in a safe environment at all times. We wish teachers well in pursuing other suitable research projects and offer the invitation to you to share your experiences with us on ELLIE.

Conclusion

In this book we have presented ways for teachers to integrate information and communication technologies with the teaching of children's literature. We have offered increasingly complex uses of technology in this integration: from using websites by children's authors in the classroom, to immersing children in the on-line visual worlds of the palace and encouraging them to use their knowledge of literature to create literary works of their own. In Chapter 1 we outlined an explicit metalanguage for talking about text and image with children. We have demonstrated how this might be incorporated into practice in succeeding chapters when discussing a range of multi-modal versions of children's literature. Finally, we have discussed the potential of a collaborative network of teachers engaging together in the 'Middle Earth Meets the Matrix' research project, with interaction and collaboration through the ELLIE website. We are eager to examine further how knowledge about children's literature can be enhanced in on-line multi-modal social contexts, both for the children we teach, and for us as teachers and researchers. We have aimed to develop a shared language of the grammars of text and image, the affordances of technology and how it might be included in studies of children's literature. This, coupled with a shared vision of researching what classroom practices are most conducive to learning, puts us in a strong position to move forward and meet the challenges of preparing children for successful social futures, drawing on the enduring lessons from literature and the increasing affordances of ICT.

Contact details for the project

Email for access to the ELLIE forums and participation in the project through Angela Thomas: a.thomas@edfac.usyd.edu.au

Email for the owner of the Middle Earth palace, Nimue: nimue@wwns.com

References

Abbott, C. (2002) Writing the visual: the use of graphic symbols in onscreen texts, in I. Snyder (ed.) *Silicon Literacies: Communication, Innovation and Education in the Electronic Age* (pp. 31–46). London: Routledge.

Almond, D. (1998) *Skellig*. London: Hodder.

Andrews, R. (2003) ICT and literacies: a new kind of research is needed, *Literacy and Learning in the Middle Years*, 11(1), 9–13.

Astorga, C. (1999) The text-image interaction and second language learning, *Australian Journal of Language and Literacy*, 22(3), 212–33.

Aurora (2004) *Harry Potters* [On-line palace]. Available: palace://harrypotter.mutant.net:9993.

Australian Bureau of Statistics (2000) *Household Use of Information Technology* [On-line]. Australian Bureau of Statistics. Available: http://www.abs.gov.au.

Bateson, C. (2002) *Rain May and Captain Daniel*. St Lucia, Brisbane: University of Queensland Press.

Bearne, E. (2000) Past perfect and future conditional: the challenge of new texts, in G. Hodges, M. Drummond and M. Styles (eds) *Tales, Tellers and Texts* (pp. 145–56). London: Continuum.

Bentley, C. (ed.) (1982) *Othello*. Sydney: Sydney Uni Press.

Berger, J. (1972) *Ways of Seeing*. New York: Penguin Books.

Blackwood, M. (1997) *Derek the Dinosaur*. Adelaide: Omnibus.

Browne, A. (1983) *Gorilla*. London: Julia MacRae.

Browne, A. (1986) *Piggybook*. London: Julia MacRae.

Browne, A. (1994) *Zoo*. London: Random House.

Browne, A. (1998) *Voices in the Park*. London: Doubleday.

Bruckman, A. (1994a) *MOOSE Crossing: Creating a Learning Culture* [On-line]. Available: http://ftp.game.org/pub/mud/text/research/moose_crossing.txt.

Bruckman, A. (1994b) *Programming for Fun: MUDs as a Context for Collaborative Learning* [On-line]. Available: http://www.cc.gatech.edu/~asb/old/ papers-index-deco1.html#NECC.

Bruckman, A. (1997) *MOOSE Crossing: Construction, Community and Learning in a Networked Virtual World for Kids* [On-line]. Available: http://www. cc.gatech.edu/fac/asb/thesis/download.html.

Buckingham, D. (2000) *After the Death of Childhood: Growing up in the Age of Electronic Media*. Cambridge: Polity Press.

Burnett, F.H. (1992) *The Secret Garden*. London: Sainsbury Walker.

Burningham, J. (1977) *Come Away from the Water, Shirley*. London: Cape.

Burningham, J. (1984) *Granpa*. London: Penguin/Puffin.

Burrell, C. and Trushell, J. (1997) 'Eye-candy' in 'interactive books' – a wholesome diet? *Reading*, 31(2), 3–6.

Callow, J. (1999) *Image Matters*. Newtown: PETA.

Callow, J. and Zammit, K. (2002) Visual literacy: from picture books to electronic texts, in M. Monteith (ed.) *Teaching Primary Literacy with ICT* (pp. 188–201). Buckingham: Open University Press.

Cannon, J. (1996) *Stellaluna*. San Francisco: LivingBooks/Random House/ Broderbund.

Carle, E. (1985) *The Very Busy Spider*. London: Penguin.

Carmody, I. and Woolman, S. (2001) *Dreamwalker*. Melbourne: Lothian.

Carroll, J. (1996) *Billy the Punk*. Milsons Point, NSW: Red Fox.

Carroll, L. (2000) *Alice's Adventures in Wonderland* (CD-ROM). Brighton: Joriko Interactive.

Casey, T. (2003) *Building Stories, Telling Games #55: Interlude: Moments of Character* [On-line]. Available: http://www.skotos.net/articles.

Caswell, B. (1990) *Meryll of the Stones*. Brisbane: University of Queensland Press.

Chambers, A. (1983) *The Present Takers*. London: Bodley Head.

Chambers, A. (1985a) Tell me: are children critics? In A. Chambers (ed.) *Booktalk*. London: Bodley Head.

Chambers, A. (1985b) *Booktalk*. London: Bodley Head.

Chaplin, E. (1994) *Sociology and Visual Representation*. London: Routledge.

Clarke, B. (2000–2004) *Look and Read – Spywatch* [On-line]. Available: http:// www.lookandread.fsnet.co.uk/stories/spy/

Cleary, B. (1976) *Ramona the Pest*. Harmondsworth: Puffin.

Cleary, B. (1978) *Ramona the Brave*. Harmondsworth: Puffin.

Cleary, B. (1981) *Ramona and her Father*. Harmondsworth: Puffin.

Cleary, B. (1982) *Ramona and her Mother*. Harmondsworth: Puffin.

Cleary, B. (1984) *Ramona Quimby, Age 8*. Harmondsworth: Puffin.

Cleary, B. (1986) *Ramona Forever*. Harmondsworth: Puffin.

Cope, B. and Kalantzis, M. (eds) (2000) *Multiliteracies: Literacy learning and the Design of Social Futures*. South Yarra: Macmillan.

Cucik, D. (2001) *The History of MUDs, Part 1* (January 2001) [On-line]. Available: http://www.archive.gamespy.com/articles/january01/muds1/.

Daniels, H. (2002) *Literature Circles: Voice and Choice in the Student-Centered Classroom* (2nd edn). Portland, Maine: Stenhouse Publications.

DartMUD (2004) *Welcome to DartMUD: The Lands of Fedarchi* [On-line]. Available: http://www.dartmud.com/.

de Saint-Exupéry, A. (2000) *The Little Prince* [CD-ROM]. Tivola.

Debord, G. (1977) *Society of the Spectacle*. Detroit, MI: Black and White.

Disney (1998) *Mulan Animated Storybook* [CD-ROM]. Burbank, CA: Disney Interactive.

Doonan, J. (1993) *Looking at Pictures in Picture Books*. Stroud: Thimble Press.

Dresang, E. (1999) *Radical Change: Books for Youth in a Digital Age*. New York: Wilson.

Dresang, E. and McClelland, K. (1999) Radical change: digital age literature and learning, *Theory into Practice*, 38(3), 160–7.

Droga, L. and Humphrey, S. (2002) *Getting Started with Functional Grammar*. NSW: Target Texts.

Dudfield, A. (1992) Children's heightened language through experiential drama. Unpublished MEd, University of Tasmania, Launceston.

Dudfield, A. (1998) Cyberliteracies: implications for education, *On-CALL*, 12(3), 15–34.

Dudfield, A. (1999) *Literacy and Cyberculture* [On-line]. International Reading Association. Available: http://www.readingonline.org/articles/dudfield/.

Early, M. (1998) *Romeo and Juliet*: New York: Harry N. Abrams.

Education Queensland (1995) *English 1–10Syllabus: A Guide to Analysing Texts*. Brisbane: Queensland Government Printing Office.

Ellis, D. (2000) *Parvana*. Sydney: Allen and Unwin.

Fienberg, A. and Gamble, K. (1998) *Minton Goes Flying*. St Leonards: Allen and Unwin.

Fleischman, P. (1998) *Whirligig*. New York: Holt.

Fleming, F. (1997) *Greek Gazette*. London: Usborne.

Fox, M. and Vivas, J. (1983) *Possum Magic*. Adelaide: Omnibus.

Freebody, P. and Luke, A. (1990) Literacies programs: debates and demands in cultural context, *Prospect*, 5, 7–16.

French, J. (1997) *Soldier on the Hill*. Sydney: HarperCollins.

Gaarder, J. (*c*.1997) *Sophie's World* [CD-ROM]. London: Marshall Media.

Gee, J. (1999) *An Introduction to Discourse Analysis*. New York: Routledge.

Goetschi, E. (1999–2004) *Meetpoint* [On-line palace]. Available: palace://braunschweig.ch:9998.

Halliday, M. (1975) *Learning How to Mean: Explorations in the Development of Language*. London: Edward Arnold.

Halliday, M.A.K. (1994) *An Introduction to Functional Grammar* (2nd edn). London: Edward Arnold.

Harvey, D. (1989) *The Condition of Postmodernity: An Inquiry into the Origins of Social Change*. Oxford: Blackwell.

Hatfield, L. (2004) *The EBBS Gallery of Client Software for MUDs and/or MOOs* [On-line]. Available: http://ebbs.english.vt.edu/mudmoo.clients.html.

Heath, S.B. (1982) What no bed time story means: narrative skills at home and school, *Language in Society*, 11, 49–76.

Hinchman, K., Alvermann, D., Boyd, F., Brozo, W. and Vacca, R. (2004) Supporting older students' in- and out-of-school literacies, *Journal of Adolescent and Adult Literacy*, 47(4), 304–11.

Hollindale, P. (1995) Children's literature in an age of multiple literacies, *The Australian Journal of Language and Literacy*, 18(4), 248–58.

Hutchins, P. (1978) *Don't Forget the Bacon*. Harmondsworth: Puffin.

Jay, M. (2002) That visual turn: the advent of visual culture, *Journal of Visual Culture*, 1(1), 87–92.

Jenks, C. (ed.) (1995) *Visual Culture*. London: Routledge.

Jennings, P. (1987) *Quirky Tales*. Ringwood, VIC: Puffin.

Jennings, P. and Gleitzman, M. (1998) *WIcked! All Six Books in One*. Ringwood, Victoria: Puffin.

Jenson, V. and Adamson, A. (Directors) (2001) *Shrek* Dreamworks.

Jinks, C. (2000) *What's Hector McKerrow Doing These Days?* Sydney: Pan Macmillan.

Johnson, N. and Giorgis, C. (2000) Discussing text and illustration with others, *The Reading Teacher*, 54(1), 109–11.

Joyce, W. (c1994) *George Shrinks* [CD-ROM]. New York: HarperCollins Interactive.

Kamil, M., Mosenthal, P., Pearson, P. and Barr, R. (eds) (2000) *Handbook of Reading Research* (vol. III). London: Lawrence Erlbaum Associates.

Katz, J. (1997) *Virtuous Reality: How America Surrendered Discussion of Moral Values to Opportunists, Nitwits and Blockheads like William Bennett*. New York: Random House.

Kidd, D. (2000) *Two Hands Together*. Ringwood: Penguin.

Knobel, M. (1999) *Everyday Literacies: Students, Discourse and Social Practice* (vol. 80). New York: Peter Lang.

Knowles, M. and Malmkjaer, K. (1996) *Language and Control in Children's Literature*. London: Routledge.

Kress, G. and van Leeuwen, T. (1996) *Reading Images: A Grammar of Visual Design*. London: Routledge.

Kress, G. and van Leeuwen, T. (2001) *Multimodal Discourse*. London: Arnold.

Labbo, L. and Reinking, D. (2000) Once upon an electronic story time, *The New Advocate*, 13(1), 25–32.

Landow, G. (1998) *The Cyberspace and Critical Theory Overview* [On-line]. Available: http://www.stg.brown.edu/projects/hypertext/landow/cspace/cspaceov.html.

Lankshear, C. and Knobel, M. (2003) New technologies, *Journal of Early Childhood Literacy*, 3(1), 59–82.

Lankshear, C. and Snyder, I. (2000) *Teachers and Technoliteracy: Managing Literacy, Technology and Learning in Schools*. Sydney: Allen and Unwin.

Lawrence, E. T. (1987) *Glory Road: Epic Romance as an Allegory of 20th Century History: The World Through the Eyes of J.R.R. Tolkien* [On-line]. Yale, New Haven Teachers Institute. Available: http://www.yale.edu/ynhti/curriculum/units/1987/2/87.02.11.x.html.

Layke (2004) *Bloody Brilliant* [On-line palace]. Available: palace://darkrain.palacebox.com:9999.

Lemke, J.L. (1998) Metamedia literacy: transforming meanings and media, in D. Reinking, M.C. McKenna, L.D. Labbo and R.D. Kieffer (eds) *Handbook of Literacy and Technology: Transformations in a Post-typographical World*. New Jersey: Lawrence Erlbaum Associates.

Lewin, C. (2000) Exploring the effects of talking book software in UK primary classrooms, *Journal of Research on Reading*, 23(2): 149–57.

Lewis, D. (2001) *Reading Contemporary Picturebooks*. London: RoutledgeFalmer.

Lonsdale, M. (1993) Postmodernism and the picture book, *English in Australia*, 103, 25–35.

Macaulay, D. (1990) *Black and White*. Boston: Houghton Mifflin.

Macken-Horarik, M. (1996) Literacy and learning across the curriculum: towards a model of register for secondary school teachers, in R. Hasan and G. Williams (eds) *Literacy in Society*. Harlow: Addison-Wesley Longman.

Mackey, M. (1994) The new basics: learning to read in a multimedia world, *English in Education*, 28(1), 9–19.

Mackey, M. (1999) Playing the phase space, *Signal*, 88, 16–33.

Mackey, M. (2002) *Literacies Across Media: Playing the Text*. London: Falmer Press.

Marsden, J. (1995) *Cool School: You Make it Happen*. Sydney: Pan Macmillan Australia.

Marsden, J. and Tan, S. (1998) *The Rabbits*. Melbourne: Lothian.

Martin, J.R. (1992) *English Text: System and Structure*. Amsterdam: Benjamins.

Martin, J.R. and Rose, D. (2003) *Working with Discourse: Meaning Beyond the Clause* (1 edn, vol. 1). London: Continuum.

Matthiessen, C. (1995) *Lexicogrammatical Cartography: English Systems*. Tokyo: International Language Sciences.

Maykitten. (2004) *Hogwarts* [On-line Palace]. Available: palace://potterchat. com:9998.

McCallum, R. (1999) Very advanced texts: metafictions and experimental work, in P. Hunt (ed.) *Understanding Children's Literature* (pp. 138–50). London and New York: Routledge.

McDonald, M. (1999) *The Binna Binna Man*. St. Leonards, NSW: Allen and Unwin.

McGee, C. (1998) *Book Raps: An internet Curriculum-Based Project*. Roseville College, Sydney: Association of Independent Schools Teacher Librarians.

McNaughton, C. (1997) *Boo!* London: HarperCollins.

MCLI (1998–2004) *Pack Your Bags for the Hero's Journey* [On-line]. Maricopa Centre for Learning and Instruction. Available: http://www.mcli.dist.maricopa.edu/smc/journey/.

Medwell, J. (1998) The talking books project: some further insights into the use of talking books to develop reading, *Reading* 32(1): 3–8.

Meek, M. (1988) *How Texts Teach What Readers Learn*. Stroud: Thimble Press.

Miller, L. (2000, September) Matilda: Finland's telematic literature project. *Reading On-line*, 4(3). Available: http://www.readingonline.org/international/inter_index. asp?HREF=/international/miller2/index.html.

Miller, L. and Olsen, J. (1998) Literacy research oriented toward features of technology and classrooms, in D. Reinking, M.C. McKenna, L.D. Labbo and R.D. Kieffer (eds) *Handbook of Literacy and Technology: Transformations in a Post-Typographical World* (pp. 343–60). New Jersey: Lawrence Erlbaum Associates.

Mills, G.E. (2003) *Action Research: A Guide for the Teacher Researcher*. New Jersey: Merrill Prentice Hall.

Mirzeoff, N. (2001) *An Introduction to Visual Culture*. London: Routledge.

Misson, R. (1998) Telling tales out of school, in F. Christie and R. Misson (eds) *Literacy and Schooling*. London: Routledge.

Mitchell, W.J.T. (1994) *Picture Theory*. Chicago: University of Chicago Press.

Montgomery, L.M. (1999) *Anne of Green Gables* (Book and CD-Rom). Frederickton, New Brunswick: Goose Lane Editions.

Morgan, W. (1999) Heterotopics: towards a grammar of hyperlinks, paper presented at *Messenger Morphs the Media 99* Conference [On-line]. Available: http://www.wordcircuits.com/htww/morgan1.htm.

Munsch, R. (1994) *The Paper Bag Princess* (CD-ROM). Buffalo, NY: Discis.

Neelands, J. and Goode, T. (2000) *Structuring Drama Word: A Handbook of Available Forms in Theatre and Drama*. Cambridge: Cambridge University Press.

Netlibris (1996–2004) *Netlibris.net – Virtual Literature Circles* [On-line]. Available: http://www.netlibris.net/international/.

Newburger, E. (2000) *Home Computers and internet Users in the United States, August 2000* [On-line]. Available: http://www.landview.census.gov/prod/2001pubs/p23–207.pdf.

New London Group (1996) A pedagogy of multiliteracies: designing social futures, *Harvard Educational Review*, 66(1), 60–91.

New South Wales Board of Studies (ed.) (1997) *Big Mob Dreaming – The Bunyip*. Sydney: Board of Studies NSW and NSW Department of School Education.

New South Wales Board of Studies (1998) *English K-6 Syllabus and Support Documents*. Sydney: New South Wales Government.

Nodelman, P. (1988) *Words about Pictures: The Narrative Art of Children's Picture Books*. Athens, GA: University of Georgia Press.

Norris, S. (2002) The implications of visual research for discourse analysis: transcription beyond language, *Visual Communication*, 1(1), 97–121.

Olondriz Ortigas, I. and Unsworth, L. (forthcoming) Exploring the narrative art of David Weisner in the context of literary and literacy pedagogy on the World Wide Web.

O'Neill, C. (1995) *Drama Worlds: A Framework for Process Drama*. New York: Heinemann.

Ormerod, J. (1985) *The Story of Chicken Licken*. London: Walker Books.

Ottley, M. (1997) *Mrs Millie's Painting*. Sydney: Hodder Headline.

Parker, T. (1997–2004) South Park, in T. Parker and M. Stone (Producers), *South Park*. Canada: Comedy Central.

Phillips, L. and Jorgensen, M. (2002) *Discourse Analysis as Theory and Method*. London: Sage.

Potter, B. (1987) *The Tale of Peter Rabbit*. Harmondsworth: Penguin.

Prain, V. (1998) Picture books in secondary English, in A. Goodwyn (ed.) *Literary and Media Texts in Secondary English* (pp. 81–97). London: Cassell.

Prain, V. and Lyons, L. (2000) ICT in English: the Australian perspective, in A. Goodwyn (ed.) *English in the Digital Age: Information and Communications Technology and the Teaching of English* (pp. 53–68). London and New York: Cassell.

Prosser, J. (ed.) (2001) *Image-Based Research: A Sourcebook for Qualitative Researchers.* London: Routledge Falmer Publications.

Pullman, P. (1989) *Spring-Heeled Jack: A Story of Bravery and Evil.* London: Corgi Yearling.

RAGTime (2002) *Middle Earth* [On-line]. Available: http://www.middleearth.com/.

Random-House. (2004) *Teachers Guide: The Hobbit* [On-line]. Random House. Available: http://www.randomhouse.com/highschool/guides/hobbit.html.

RandomHouse/Broderbund (1994) *Arthur's Teacher Trouble* [CD-ROM]. San Francisco: Living Books/RandomHouse/Broderbund.

Ravelli, L. (2000) Getting started with functional analysis of texts, in L. Unsworth (ed.) *Researching Language in Schools and Communities: Functional Linguistic Perspectives* (pp. 27–64). London: Cassell.

Rose, G. (2001) *Visual Methodologies.* London: Sage.

Rowling, J.K. (1999) *Harry Potter and the Sorcerer's Stone* [CD-ROM] (unabridged). New York: Listening Library/Random House.

Rowling, J.K. (1999) *Harry Potter and the Prisoner of Azkaban.* London: Bloomsbury.

Sacher, L. (1998) *Holes.* New York: Farrar, Straus and Giroux.

Sanchez (II), E. and Myrick, D. (1999) *The Blair Witch Project*: Artisan Entertainment.

Scieszka, J. and Johnson, S. (1991) *The Frog Prince Continued.* New York: Viking Kestrel.

Scieszka, J. and Smith, L. (1992) *The Stinky Cheese Man and Other Fairly Stupid Tales.* New York: Viking.

Sendak, M. (1962) *Where the Wild Things Are.* London: The Bodley Head.

Shattered Kingdoms. (2004) *Aster* [On-line]. Available: http://www. shattered-kingdoms.org/hero_aster.

Simpson, A. (2004). Book Raps as online multimodal communication: towards a model of interactive pedagogy. *International Journal of Learning*, 10, 2705–2714.

SkotosGamingandStorytellingCommunity. (2004) *The Eternal City* [On-line]. Available: http://www.skotos.net/games/eternal-city/.

Snyder, I. and Joyce, M. (1998) *Page to Screen: Taking Literacy into the Electronic Era.* London: Routledge.

Sorenson, L. (2000–2004) *Middle Earth* [On-line palace]. Available: palace://middleearthpalace.com:9998; http://middleearthpalace.com:9984/palace/client/ instantpal.html.

Souza, A. (2004) *Nexus Quest* [On-line palace]. Available: palace:/fantasia.org:9998.

Stake, R. (1995) *The Art of Case Study Research.* London: Sage.

Steig, W. (1990) *Shrek.* New York: Michael Di Capua Books.

Stephens, J. (2000) Modality and space in picture book art: Allen Say's *Emma's Rug, CREArTA*, 1(1), 45–59.

Stephens, J. and Watson, K. (eds) (1994) *From Picture Book to Literary Theory*. Sydney: St Clair Press.

Stringer, E. (2004) *Action Research in Education*. New Jersey: Pearson Prentice Hall.

Stubbs, J. (1999) Book raps: an internet project, in L. Hay and J. Henri (eds) *The Net Effect*. London: The Scarecrow Press Inc.

Styles, M. and Arizpe, E. (2001) 'A gorilla with Grandpa's eyes': how children interpret visual texts – A case study of Anthony Browne's "Zoo", *Children's Literature in Education*, 32(4), 261–81.

Suler, J. (1996) *One of Us: Participant Observation Research at the Palace* [On-line]. Available: http://www.rider.edu/users/suler/psycyber/partobs.html.

Summer Rain, M. (1993) *Dreamwalker: The Path of Sacred Power*. Charlottesville, VA: Hampton Roads Publishing.

Taylor, P. (2000) *Drama Classroom: Action, Reflection, Transformation*. New York: Falmer Press.

Teale, W.H. and Sulzby, E. (1987) Literacy acquisition in early childhood: the roles of access and mediation in storybook reading, in D.A. Wagner (ed.) *The Future of Literacy in a Changing World* (pp. 111–30). New York: Pergamon Press.

Thomas, A. (1999–2003) *Kids, Enfants, Kinder!* [On-line palace]. Available: palace://kek.palaceplanet.com:8080.

Thomas, A. (2001) The cyber child, *disClosure: A Journal of Social Theory*, Vol. 10, Special Issue: Childhood, pp. 143–75.

Thomas, A. (2002–2004) *Electronic Literature and Literacies in International Education (ELLIE)* [On-line]. Available: http://sirius.linknet.com.au/ellie/index.html.

Tolkien, J.R.R. (1937) *The Hobbit*. London: George Allen and Unwin.

Tolkien, J.R.R. (1955) *The Return of the King: Being the Third Part of The Lord of the Rings*. London: George Allen and Unwin.

Trushell, J., Burrell, C. and Maitland, A. (2001) Year 5 pupils reading an 'Interactive Storybook' on CD-ROM: losing the plot? *British Journal of Educational Technology*, 32(4), 389–401.

Underwood, J. (2000) A comparison of two types of computer support for reading development, *Journal of Research in Reading*, 23(2), 136–48.

Unsworth, L. (2001) *Teaching Multiliteracies Across the Curriculum: Changing Contexts of Text and Image in Classroom Practice*. Buckingham: Open University Press.

Unsworth, L. (2003a) Comparing image/text relations in conventional book and electronic versions of well-known literary texts for children: from semiotic analysis to classroom practice, paper presented at the 8th Conference of the International Federation of Teachers of English (IFTE): 'Transforming literacies – changing English', University of Melbourne, 5–8 July.

Unsworth, L. (2003b) Re-framing research and practice relating to CD-ROM narratives in classroom literacy learning: addressing 'radical change' in digital age literature for children, *Issues in Educational Research*, 13(2), 55–70.

Unsworth, L. (2003c) Describing the recontextualization in electronic format of images in illustrated literary narratives for children: exploring possible systemic approaches. Paper presented at the Australian Systemic Functional Linguistics Association Conference, Adelaide, 17–19 July.

Unsworth, L. and Wheeler, J. (2002) Re-valuing the role of images in reviewing picture books, *Reading: Language and Literacy*, 36(2), 68–74.

Van Allsburg, C. (1981) *Jumanji*. Boston: Houghton Mifflin.

Van Allsburg, C. (1997) *The Polar Express* (CD-ROM). Somerville, MA: Houghton Mifflin Interactive.

Wagner, J. (1995) *The Werwolf Knight*. Sydney: Random House.

Walter, V. (1998) *Making up Megaboy*. New York: DK Publishing.

Watson, K. (ed.) (1997) *Word and Image*. Sydney: St Clair Press.

Watson, V. (1996) The left-handed reader in linear sentences and unmapped pictures, in V. Watson and M. Styles (eds) *Talking Pictures: Pictorial Texts and Young Readers*. London: Hodder and Stoughton.

Webster. (2004) *Webster Central School District* [On-line]. Available: http://www.websterschools.org/webpages.

Wiesner, D. (1990) *Hurricane*. New York: Clarion.

Wiesner, D. (1991) *Tuesday*. New York: Clarion.

Wiesner, D. (1992) *June 29, 1999*. New York: Clarion.

Wiesner, D. (1999) *Sector 7*. New York: Clarion.

Wiesner, D. (2001) *The Three Pigs*. New York: Clarion.

Wild, M. and Brooks, R. (2000) *Fox*. Sydney: Allen and Unwin.

Williams, G. (1977) *Reading and Talking about Novels: A Consideration of the Contribution of Peer Discussions of Novels to the Development of Inter-Personal Understanding in Upper Primary School Children*. Sydney: University of Sydney.

Williams, G. (1987) Space to play: the analyses of narrative structure in classroom work with children's literature, in M. Saxby and G. Winch (eds) *Give Them Wings: The Experience of Children's Literature* (pp. 355–68). Melbourne: Macmillan.

Williams, G. (1993) Using systemic grammar in teaching young learners: an introduction, in L. Unsworth (ed.) *Literacy Learning and Teaching: Language as Social Practice in the Primary School*. Melbourne: Macmillan.

Williams, G. (1998) Children entering literate worlds, in F. Christie and R. Misson (eds) *Literacy in Schooling* (pp. 18–46). London: Routledge.

Williams, G. (2000) Children's literature, children and uses of language description, in L. Unsworth (ed.) *Researching Language in Schools and Communities: A Functional Linguistic Perspective*. London: Cassell.

Winton, T. (1997) *Blueback*. Sydney: Pan Macmillan Australia.

Index